AIRCRAFT MONOGRAPH

ADAM SKUPIEWSKI

Fw 190 A/F/G/S

PART I

◄◄ AJ•PRESS

AIRCRAFT MONOGRAPH 4

COPYRIGHT © – A.J.–PRESS – 1996
P. O. Box 28
81–209 GDYNIA 9
POLAND
Tel. & Fax. (+48 58) 20-18-77

English Edition:

BOOKS INTERNATIONAL
69B Lynchford Road
Farnborough, Hampshire GU14 6EJ, England
Telephone: 01252-376564, Fax: 01252-370181

Editor in Chief: **Adam Jarski**
Cover painting: **Jarosław Wróbel**
Colour Plates: **Jacek Jackowski, Grzegorz Jackowski**
Book Design: **Jarosław Wróbel, A.J.–PRESS**
Translations: **Wojtek Matusiak**
Assistant Editor: **Barry Ketley**
Drawings: **Krzysztof Żurek, Witold Hazuka**
English Edition edited by: **Barry Ketley**
Printed in Poland by: **Drukarnia Oruńska**,
     Gdańsk, ul. Świętokrzyska 47, tel. (+48 58) 399351

ISBN–83–86208–35–X

Front cover: A Luftwaffe ace, Oberleutnant Werner Nowotny, Staffelkapitän 1./JG 54 lands his Fw 190 at a snow—covered airfield.
Paint: Jarosław Wróbel

BOOKS INTERNATIONAL SALES TEAM AND TERRITORIES
POLAND

BOOKS INTERNATIONAL
ul. LUBELSKA 30-32
03-808 WARSZAWA
POLAND
Tel. & Fax +48 2 2619 60 57

FRANCE, SWITZERLAND, HUNGARY, CZECH & SLOVAK REPUBLICS

Mr. Juliusz Komarnicki
CP 196
CH–6900 MASSAGNO
SWITZERLAND
Tel.: +41 - 91 - 57 15 39, Fax: +41 - 91 - 56 78 65

GREECE, ITALY, PORTUGAL, SPAIN (INC. GIB.), SLOVENIA & CROATIA

Mr. Patrick Bygate
CP 196
CH–6900 MASSAGNO
SWITZERLAND
Tel.: +41 - 91 - 57 15 39, Fax: +41 - 91 - 56 78 65

NORDIC GROUP OF COUNTRIES

Mr. Ove B. Poulsen
OPB MARKETING
Hegnet 13
DK–2600 GLOSTRUP
DENMARK
Tel. & Fax: +45 - 43 - 96 50 60

GERMANY, AUSTRIA

Mr. Robert Pleysier
Walkottelanden 72
NL-7542 ENSCHEDE
THE NETHERLANDS
Tel.: +31 - 53 - 77 53 77, Fax: +31 - 53 - 77 82 98

NATHERLANDS, BELGIUM & LUXEMBOURG

Mr. Reinier Pleysier
Kerkdijk 21
PO Box 166
NL-8180 AD HERRE
THE NETHERLANDS
Tel.: +31 - 5782 - 5203, Fax: +31 - 5782 - 5243

Fw 190 A — 0, W.Nr. 0022, SB + ID, on a factory airfield, autumn 1940

(MVT via M. Krzyżan)

The Focke — Wulf 190 was one of the best fighter aircraft of World War II. Designed and developed under Professor. Dr (Eng.) Kurt Tank, an unquestioned genius among the world's aircraft designers, the aircraft led the way in aeronautical engineering from the very beginning of its existence until the end of the war, forcing competitors to strive to their utmost to match or beat it. With a total quantity of over 20,000 produced, the aircraft gave the Luftwaffe both power and combat effectiveness.

FOCKE — WULF 190 A

Two main reasons lay behind the creation of the **Focke — Wulf 190** fighter. In the late 1930s, the arms race was running at a high rate, and the RLM (Reich Air Ministry) realised perfectly well that a single type of pure fighter (i. e. the Messerschmitt **Bf 109**) might not guarantee the Luftwaffe's leading position among the air powers. Another reason was the RLM's reaction to the intelligence reports that other powers (even smaller countries) were developing and using at least two different types of modern fighters. All this led the RLM's Technische Amt (Technical Department) to prepare, at the turn of 1937, specifications for the new fighter. In the Spring of 1938 these were sent to aircraft designers, including the Focke — Wulf Flugzeugbau AG. The team of Professor Kurt Tank and Rudolf Blaser developed a small, compact fighter, powered by an air — cooled radial engine. However, at that time the RLM decision makers preferred liquid — cooled in — line engines, and thus were not satisfied by the new design. The radial engine was said to have excessive frontal area drag and

to adversely effect the forward field of view during taxiing. However, both these argument could be disputed, since radial engines feature a number of advantages, as was proved by foreign aircraft with such power — plants. Even the obvious shortcomings could be minimised by careful positioning of the engine within the aircraft structure.

It is not impossible that lobbying by other manufacturers also played a part in the initial decision to reject the Focke — Wulf offering. Consequently, if not for a lucky coincidence, the **Fw 190** might have ended up in the wastebasket. There were two reasons why this did not happen. The first was disappointment with the **Heinkel 112** and **100** fighters which proved to be unsuitable, and were not put into production. The short

series of He 112 Bs actually built was withdrawn from Luftwaffe service and sold to Romania, while the few pre — series He 100 Ds were used briefly in 1940 for propaganda purposes to create the myth of He 113, „the latest Luftwaffe fighter" (quite successfully, as some Allied fighter pilots claimed to have shot down He 113s!).

The other reason was very simple — the two principal manufacturers of the in — line, liquid — cooled engines (i. e. Junkers at Dessau and Daimler — Benz at Stuttgart — Untertürkheim) were not be able to satisfy the demand of the aircraft manufacturers. As early as the turn of 1939 it was clear that Daimler — Benz, in spite of starting additional production lines, would be hard pressed to ensure supplies of engines for **Bf 109** and **Bf 110** fighters, as a result other

The first wooden Fw 190 mock — up. Like most such mock — ups it only had the port wing and port undercarriage unit

(MVT via M. Krzyżan)

Fw 190 V1 in the assembly hall
(MVT via M. Krzyżan)

ever, the ducted spinner proved unsatisfactory, and the engine continued to overheat. The problem was rather serious, as even during normal cruise the cockpit temperature rose above 55°C. The cockpit also needed sealing, as large amounts of exhaust gases leaked in, causing a potentially lethal danger to the pilot should he fail to wear his oxygen mask. (A similar situation to that encountered by the British **Hawker Typhoon**, itself to be built as an answer to the **Fw 190**).

After the preliminary flight testing, the aircraft was delivered to the Luftwaffe test centre at Rechlin, which also played the role of the RLM acceptance organisation. Tests there confirmed both the advantages and shortcomings of the new design. An unexpectedly high maximum speed of 595 km/h at an altitude of 4,000 m (without armament) was attained. Subsequently the aircraft was returned to the manufacturers to receive necessary modifications, mainly to the cooling system. In the case of a radial engine the only way was to intensify the air flow. This was achieved by adding a 10—blade fan on the propeller shaft, in front of the engine, at the front of the cowling. The ducted spinner was replaced with a conventional small one that only covered the hub of the VDM propeller (a Hamilton—Standard propeller was also tested). Wind—tunnel testing proved that the large spinner did not ensure the necessary air flow, while its influence on the aerodynamic drag was negligible. This modification improved cooling efficiency, although the engine continued to work at a high range of temperatures. In the meantime the aircraft received a military, instead of civil registration.First it was WL—FOLY, then FO+LY.

In the autumn 1939 construction of the second prototype, the **Fw 190V2**, W.Nr. 0002, FO+LZ, was completed and it was first flown on 31 October. This machine received the fanned engine, and an armament of two 7,9 mm Rheinmetall—Borsig MG 17 and two 13 mm MG 131 machine guns in the inboard portions of the wings. Firing trials were carried out at the Tarnewitz proving grounds. On January 25, 1940, after another re—registering to RM+CA (**V1**) and RM+CB (**V2**), both prototypes commenced another series of flying trials, with the aim of assessing the effect of the modifications on flying characteristics and engine cooling. The **Fw 190V2** was shown to Hermann Göring, and obviously made a good impression as testified to by the earlier than expected order for a pre—production batch of 40 **Fw 190A—0s**. Soon after, on March 4, 1940, the **V2** suffered an accident and was severely damaged, when the test—pilot, Rohlfs, overturned it during taxiing. The aircraft had accumulated a mere 50 flying hours by that time.

In the meantime the BMW company developed a newer, more promising engine

manufacturers' orders were cancelled. That was the reason why Heinkel was forced to reduce, and subsequently halt, (in 1940), production of the DB 601—powered **He 111P**, and switch to the Jumo 211—powered **He 111H**. The latter engines were only available in sufficient quantities for the **He 111**, **Ju 87** and **Ju 88** bombers. Thus, out of necessity, the project from the Bremen—based Focke—Wulf Flugzeugbau AG was accepted.

A new team, headed by Rudolf Blaser, was created to develop the new fighter. It included Willi Käther, Ludwig Mittelhuber and Andreas von Fählmann, the chief of the design office (at that time Kurt Tank was the company's technical manager). Work started and advanced quickly, following the RLM—issued preliminary order for four prototypes. First, a wooden mock—up was constructed, and in the autumn of 1938 prototype construction commenced. The new aircraft was a low—wing cantilever monoplane of an all—metal, semi—monocoque structure, with retractable

landing gear. At first it was planned to use the BMW 139 18—cylinder double—radial engine. This was a new design from the BMW company, combining two 9—cylinder BMW 132 engines. Even though the engine would greatly reduce forward visibility on the ground, it was rated at 1,550 HP (1,140 kW) maximum output, thus being 25% more powerful than the in—line DB 601 or Jumo 211, with greater resistance to battle—damage.

High power output gave rise to serious problems with cooling, and a special ducted spinner was developed (used on the first prototype, **Fw 190V1**, W.Nr. 0001), to improve and intensify cooling air flow while reducing drag. The prototype, completed by late Spring 1939, was registered as D—OPZE and, after the preliminary ground trials, was first flown by Hans Sander (Focke—Wulf's chief test pilot) on June 1, 1939. First trials proved the flying characteristics of the new aircraft to be excellent, including controls sensitivity, even though the ailerons needed to be improved. How-

Fw 190 V1 in the assembly hall, the original version with the ducted propeller hub
(MVT via M. Krzyżan)

Above and right: Hans Sander at the controls of Fw 190 V1, W. Nr. 0001.

(MVT via M. Krzyżan)

— the BMW 801 14—cylinder, double—row, radial unit. The decision was taken to concentrate on the new design and stop any further work on the unsuccessful BMW 139. Even though the new powerplant was similar in diameter, it was longer and heavier. Therefore, the Blaser team faced a substantial redesign of the airframe to accept the new engine. At that time two further prototypes, the **Fw 190V3** and **V4**, were nearing completion. The decision was taken to abandon them, and start work on a new aircraft, the **Fw 190V5**, designed from the outset for the BMW 801 engine. The **Fw 190V3** would be cannibalised for spare parts, while the **V4** would be used for structural ground—testing. The greater weight of the BMW 801, as well as the planned use of many different armament configurations, necessitated strengthening the entire airframe. The fuselage structure was stiffened, and the cockpit was repositioned further aft. The latter modification served to solve the cockpit overheating problems and allowed more space for a fuselage armament bay. On the other hand this led to slight reduction in cockpit space, but thanks to the excellent arrangement of the controls this proved to have only a minor effect. Also the rear part of the cockpit canopy was modified with duralumin replacing some of the transparent area. The only negative effect of the cockpit repositioning was a fur-

Prototype Fw 190 V1 during an official presentation in the summer 1939. In the foreground is General Ernst Udet, Chief of the RLM Technical Dept. (centre). To his left Ing. Lucht, to his right, Ing. Carl Francke

(MVT via M. Krzyżan)

Fw 190 V1 prototype, W.Nr. 0001, FO+LY, after the modification.

(MVT via M. Krzyżan)

ther reduction in forward visibility during taxiing.

The rudder outline was slightly changed, and the trim tab was replaced with a ground−adjusted metal panel. The expected substantial increase in weight (by more than 25%) also necessitated undercarriage strengthening. Thus new, stronger main legs were used, the hydraulic retraction system was replaced with an electric one, and larger wheels with new, flat covers were used. To accommodate the new land-ing gear in the wing, the undercarriage bays were enlarged by moving the inboard wing leading edge further forward.

The **Fw 190V5**, W.Nr. 0005, powered by the BMW 801C−0 engine, was first flown in early spring of 1940. After a series of comparative trials against the **V1** it was found that the weight increase affected flying characteristics, which would clearly get worse in the future as the design would inevitably acquire more armament and equipment. Thus, the wing also needed redesign, as increasing the wing area would improve the performance. This was achieved by a slight increase in wing span and moving the leading edge forward. A new wing was thus created, with an area of 18.30 sq. m, span of 10.506 m and an un-changed airfoil. The tailplane was also modified, with a span of 3.650 m. Shortly afterwards the tailplane area was also en-larged by moving the leading edge forward. The new wing was to be tested on another prototype, but it was finally fitted to the **V5**, when in August of 1940 Hans Sander damaged its wing during a force−landing after the engine cowling opened in flight. So modified, the prototype was called **V5g** (g=grösser − larger), while in any refer-ence to the previous standard the name of **V5k** (k=kleiner − smaller) was used. As proved by flight−testing, the new wing only reduced the top speed by 10 km/h, while greatly improving the flying characteristics, especially climbing speed.

Fw 190 V1 prototype, W.Nr. 0001, FO+LY, after the modification. The small orthodox propeller spinner is clearly visible

(MVT via M. Krzyżan)

In October of 1940 the first two **Fw 190A−0**s were completed, receiving proto-type designations of **Fw 190V6**, W.Nr. 0006, and **Fw 190V7**. Both aircraft featured the older, small wing, since the production line was started before the design work on the new wing was completed. Consequently, the first 9 aircraft were completed to the earlier standard, while the new wing was first intro-duced on W.Nr. 0015. Therefore the two prototypes and the first seven **Fw 190A−0**s featured the smaller wing. In parallel with the new wing, the new, larger fin and rudder

Incomplete equipment in the cockpit of Fw 190 V5k during fitting. Note the experimentally fitted (behind the lower control panel) filter and valve set for the fuel system, equipped with an additional hand pump lever. Such pump was not used on production aircraft, and the unit was placed outside the cockpit, on the outer side of the fireproof bulkhead.

(MVT via M. Krzyżan)

was introduced, while the new tailplane was only fitted starting from the **A – 2** model. The **Fw 190V6** was used for extensive performance and flying trials, while the **Fw 190V7** served for armament testing. The new weapons fit consisted of four MG 17s and two 20 mm Rheinmetall – Borsig (Oerlikon licence) MG FF cannon. The latter were fitted in the wings, just outboard of the landing gear attachment points. After firing trials at Tarnewitz, this armament set was used as a temporary standard for the **A – 1** series aircraft. It was to be superseded by a new one, with two 20 mm Mauser MG 151/20 E cannon replacing the wing mounted MG 17 guns, as soon as the new synchronising unit (to fire through the propeller disc) was introduced into series production. As of November 1940 the first **Fw 190A – 0s** deliveries commenced, the aircraft starting with W.Nr 0010 featuring BMW 801C – 1 engines instead of the pre – production **C – 0**. Of the 40 aircraft ordered, only 28 were actually built (up to W.Nr. 0035), most of which were later converted to prototypes for testing of various gun and bomb armament systems. Several aircraft were also used for tests of new engine variants and various equipment. For example, during summer 1943 the **Fw 190A – 0** W.Nr. 0021, SB+IE, was used at Langenhagen in trials of a powder – cartridge ejection seat, carried out by Hans Sander. Depending on the type of modification these aircraft received either the prototype V designation, or the U (Umrüstbausatz) suffix. Many U – modifications for the **Fw 190A – 0** are known (U1 to U13), which were applied to one or more aircraft, but the limited space of this work does not allow detailed study.

According to the invoice for the last 15 large wing **Fw 190A – 0s** (as submitted to the RLM) one aircraft cost 152,400 RM.

Before the production of the **Fw 190A – 1**, the first series version, was started, many minor shortcomings had to be cured, and handling/maintenance experience in field conditions gained. This is why a team of air and ground crew was selected from II./JG 26, and these formed Erprobungsstaffel 190, a special test flight. This unit, under Technical Officer Oberleutnant Otto Behrens, received six **Fw 190A – 0s** (W.Nr. 0013, 0014, 0018, 0019, 0021, 0022). These were used for initial training, led by Rechlin specialists, flying taking place from the Rechlin – Roggenthin airfield. Subsequently the unit was moved to Le Bourget near Paris (France). Extensive trials showed that the BMW 801 power plant suffered from frequent malfunctions, and also that it had a continuous tendency to overheating, especially the rear row of cylinders. This mainly occurred on the ground, after prolonged periods of low – revs operation,

when the cooling airflow was minimal. The engine's Kommandogerät (automatic control unit) caused many problems, as did the new VDM variable – pitch propeller. In some cases fuel and oil systems leaked, and the spark plugs were subject to excessive wear. Engine cowlings had a tendency to open up in the air, as a result of poor lock design. Emergency jettisoning of the cockpit hood proved difficult , especially at speeds of more than 250 km/h, which resulted from the aerodynamic flow pressing the canopy against the fuselage. This was cured with a small explosive cartridge to blow the canopy off. The wide range of shortcomings caused a special committee to arrive at Le Bourget, which decided that the testing should be stopped until all defects could be removed. After some 50 modifications were introduced, the RLM agreed to accept the Fw 190 for Luftwaffe service. The Focke – Wulf company received an order for 100 **Fw 190A – 1** fighters and an option for further contracts. It was clear that, apart from Focke – Wulf, other companies would undertake licence production. At first, the

lines at Bremen and Marienburg (now Malbork in Poland) Focke – Wulf factories were started up. Arado at Warnemnde and AGO at Ochersleben would be the first **Fw 190** licence – manufacturers.

Focke – Wulf 190A – 1

The initial **Fw 190A – 1** left the Focke – Wulf Marienburg factory in June 1941, and by August the monthly output had reached 30 aircraft. During this latter month the Warnemünde Arado factory started deliveries, and in October AGO at Ochersleben joined the team. This allowed 82 aircraft to enter service with the Luftwaffe by late September, and the full order, in fact 102 aircraft, was delivered by the end of October. One of these, designated **Fw 190A – 1/U1**, received a trial installation of the new BMW 801D – 2 engine variant. Some **Fw 190A – 1s**, just like several **A – 0s**, received FuG 25 IFF besides the standard FuG 7a R/T set.

Engine overheating and fires continued to be the main topics in Technical Officers' reports. All production aircraft received ar-

An **Fw 190 A—0.** Note the spinner with one section painted white.

(MVT via M. Krzyżan)

mouring of the cockpit, oil tank and cooler, as standard.

Focke-Wulf 190A-2

The **Fw 190A—2** was the second production version, and was powered with the improved BMW 801C—2. It was this model that finally disposed of the rear engine block overheating problem, achieved by adding cooling slots at the rear sides of engine cowling. These cooling vents were retrofitted on most **Fw 190A—1s** in service. Deliveries of the new synchronising gear allowed the introducion of 20 mm Mauser MG 151/20E wing cannon (instead of MG 17 guns). This change forced a slight 'bulging' of the upper armament covers at the wing roots, and increased the AUW to 3,850 kg. Revi C/12C gunsights were replaced with Revi C/12D. A new, more efficient undercarriage retraction system was introduced. **Fw 190**

airframes, starting from the **A—2** variant, featured under-fuselage attachments for the ETC 501 bomb rack, but so far no confirmation was found as to whether the device was actually fitted on any A—2s. One aircraft, W.Nr. 120315, CM+CN, designated **Fw 190A—2/U1**, was experimentally fitted with an auto-pilot. Some sources also quote a reconnaissance version called A—2/U3.

A total of 420 **Fw 190A—2** were produced.

Focke-Wulf 190A-3

BMW 801D—2 engine series production started in the Spring of 1942, to be introduced on all the **Fw 190** production lines and led to the creation of a new variant, the **Fw 190A—3.** The increased power output of the BMW 801D—2 (rated at 1,730 HP) was achieved by increasing both the compression ratio in cylinders and the low and high speeds of the two-speed supercharger. Greater compression and supercharging pressure necessitated use of 96-octane C3 fuel, instead of the used 87-octane B4 fuel used before.

Standard **Fw 190A—3s** were armed similarly to the previous variants. However, starting from this version, the A airframes were widely used in extensive development programmes aimed at optimising armament and equipment systems, to increase the **Fw 190**'s operational capabilities, and use in non-fighter roles. Most modifications were standardised as Umrüstbausatz sets, although some were not, and these can only be recognised in photos. No data regarding numbers of conversions are available. The most widely known are the **Fw 190A—3** with ETC 501 rack under the fuselage, capable of carrying up to 500 kg bombs (1 x 500 kg, 1 x 250 kg or 4 x 50 kg on an ER 4 adapter) or a 300 l drop tank for long-range fighters. Some aircraft used in the pure fighter role (without racks) had their armament reduced by removing the wing MG FF cannon, and this was not indicated by any additional designation. Furthermore, 72 **Fw 190 Aa—3** were manufactured (a=ausländisch — foreign), and exported to Turkey between October 1942 and March 1943. Most were fitted with A—1 standard armament, i. e. 4 x MG 17 plus 2 x MG FF, and the radio equipment lacked (needless to say) the FuG 25.

Apart from the above mentioned changes, the following Umrüstbausatz modification sets were developed for the **Fw 190A—3** and the subsequent variants. It should be pointed out here, however, that in many cases these were merely projects, never implemented or only experimental installations on one or two aircraft.

Fw 190 A—0s in the final assembly hall. Weapon elements have been retouched from the photo by a wartime censor.

(MVT via M. Krzyżan)

Pre series Fw 190 A—0s and the Fw 190 V1 (second from left) on the factory airfield at Bremen in mid—1940.

(MAP)

- **Fw 190A—3/U1** — one test aircraft (W.Nr. 130270, PG+GY) with 15 cm longer engine mounting; served as a prototype for the **Fw 190A—5**.
- **Fw 190A—3/U2** — armed with 73 mm RZ 65 rocket missile launchers inside wings (three in each wing), tested on W.Nr. 130386.
- **Fw 190A—3/U3** — reconnaissance fighter with Rb 50/30 and Rb 75/30 cameras in the fuselage; MG FF cannon removed; only one aircraft.
- **Fw 190A—3/U4** — reconnaissance fighter with two Rb 12.5/7 x 9 cameras in the fuselage and EK16 cine—camera or Robot II 35 mm camera in the port wing leading edge; armament as U3; ETC 501 rack with stabilising bars for a 300 l fuel tank under the fuselage. 12 aircraft built.
- **Fw 190A—3/U7** — an attempt to create a high—altitude fighter, with reduced weight, armed with only two MG 151/20 E cannon. Only three aircraft (W.Nr. 130528, 530, and 531), easily recognisable by the external air intakes for the supercharger on both sides of the engine.

Focke—Wulf 190A—4

In July 1942 production of the **A—3** was stopped in favour of the new **Fw 190A—4**.

The main difference lay in the BMW 801D—2 variant adapted to use the MW 50 system which offered short time power increases by injecting a water/methanol (CH_3OH) 1:1 mixture. This allowed power to be boosted to 2,100 HP for up to 10 minutes (exceeding the time limit could cause serious damage to the engine). Because of the delays in MW 50 equipment manufacture, this installation was not fitted to **Fw 190A—4**s. Even though their engines could accept such a modification, it was never fitted, and the **A—8** was the first variant to actually feature such a modification as standard.

Another identifying feature of the **A—4** was the replacement of the FuG 7a R/T set with the more modern FuG 16Z. Another minor change was that the vertical attachment for the wire aerial was mounted on the fin (this facilitates identification between **A—3** and **A—4** variants, while it is often extremely difficult to differentiate **A—3** from **A—2**). Some later production **A—4**s featured another refinement in the form of movable flaps instead of slots on the rear engine cowling, which allowed the pilot to precisely adjust the engine temperature. Because of the continuous build—up of orders, more factories were included in the production programme, the Fieseler works at Kassel—Waldau among them.

Large numbers of **Fw 190A—4**s featured reduced armament, lacking the MG FF cannon. Trials with different variants of weapon systems and equipment, mainly in form of Umrüstbausatz sets, led to the creation of the following versions:
- **Fw 190A—4/U1** — fighter—bomber with an under—fuselage ETC 501 rack and no MG FF cannon. Because of insufficient deliveries of BMW 801D—2s, several dozen aircraft of this variant built in the autumn of 1943 were powered by older C—2 engines.

Fw 190 A—0s in the final assembly hall. Weapon elements in wing have been retouched from the photo by a wartime censor.

(MVT via M. Krzyżan)

- **Fw 190A–4/U3** – fighter–bomber, armed like the U1, albeit with the BMW 801D–2 engine. Aircraft for night operations had a landing light fitted in the port wing leading edge. The **A–4/U3** designation was soon changed to **F–1** and further development was carried on as the new **Fw 190F** attack version.
- **Fw 190A–4/U4** – reconnaissance fighter with two Rb 12.5/7 x 9 cameras. No MG FF cannon.
- **Fw 190A–4/U8** – long–range fighter–bomber able to carry two 300 l drop tanks under wings (on Weserflug V.Tr.– Ju 87 racks with duralumin fairings). The bomb load was carried on the ETC 501 rack under the fuselage. To reduce weight only the MG 151/20 E cannon were left as armament. This modification was the basis of the new **Fw 190G** fighter–bomber version, by becoming the **Fw 190G–1**. There was also a transitional variant (probably one aircraft only) with more modern wing drop tank attachments – the V.Mtt–Schloß.

Apart from the Umrüstbausatz, some **Fw 190A–4** featured Rüstsatz (R) sets that were simpler to install, and in some cases could be fitted at front–line units, although they required factory–mounted fittings on the airframe. It is worth noting here that the stories of their being extremely easy to install, and interchangeable between aircraft, are completely untrue. Some of the R modifications were no less complicated than the U ones, and in some cases the difference between U and R sets was purely theoretical (in fact, later on, many U variants were renamed in the R range). The first set to be widely used was two tubular launchers for air–to–air missiles, the 210 mm W.Gr. 21 used to break the defensive box USAAF bomber formations. Aircraft with this armament were called **Fw 190A–4/R6**. Some authors mention a fighter–bomber version called **Fw 190A–4/R1**, apparently with the modification consisting of the FuG 16 ZE radio set being fitted, with a *Morane*–type aerial under the port wing, to enable direct communication with ground units involved in fighting. It is true that a small number of such aircraft existed (fitted with ETC 501 racks), but whether the modification was indeed standardised as a U or R set is yet to be confirmed.

A total of more than 900 **Fw 190A–4s** was manufactured.

Focke–Wulf 190A–5

The experience gained during testing of the **Fw 190A–3/U1** led the Blaser team to the conclusion that the anticipated installation of additional equipment and armament would inevitably affect the CoG position. To counteract this, they decided to reposition the engine slightly further forward. This was done by making the steel engine mounting 15 cm longer.

The new engine mounting was to be introduced on all production lines. The change resulted in the aircraft's overall length being increased to 9.100 m and a new variant, called **Fw 190A–5**, being born. During 1942 it replaced the **A–4**. Slight modifications were also introduced in the cockpit equipment. Among others, a new electric artificial horizon and more modern oxygen system were introduced. The FuG 25a IFF was also commonly installed. The rear fuselage equipment compartment cover was enlarged and moved further aft. Standard armament remained unchanged, i. e. consisted of 2 x MG 17, 2 x MG 151/20 E and 2 x MG FF.

Thanks to suitably prepared airframes, the **Fw 190A–5** was able to accommodate many different Umrüstbausatz sets:
- **Fw 190A–5/U1** – similar (but for the engine mounting) to the A–4/U1, temporarily powered with the BMW 801C–2 engine.
- **Fw 190A–5/U2** – long–range fighter–bomber, equipped for night operations (anti–glare panels over side exhausts. ETC 501 rack for 250 and 500 kg bombs under the fuselage, additional 300 l fuel tanks under wings on V.Mtt–Schloß (Verkleidetes Messerschmitt Schloß). EK16 camera and a landing light were fitted in the

Two photographs of Fw 190 A–0s with a running engine. Above, an aircraft marked SB+...?, and below, KB+PU.

(MVT via M. Krzyżan)

leading edge. No MG FF cannon. This variant served as a basis for a night fighter with the FuG 217 *Neptun* J — 2 radar, but the number of aircraft in this version is not known (the only one known had no rack, no camera and no landing lights).

● **Fw 190A — 5/U3** — fighter — bomber with an ETC 501 rack, no MG FF cannon. After the designations were changed it was series — produced in the F — range as the **Fw 190F — 2**. It also appeared in a tropical version, with a dust — filter, known as **A — 5/U3/tp (F — 2tp)**.

● **Fw 190A — 5/U4** — reconnaissance fighter with two RB 12,5/7x9 cameras, and a reduced armament consisting of 2 x MG 17

and 2 x MG 151/20E. A tropical variant, called **A — 5/U4/tp**, also existed.

● **Fw 190A — 5/U8** — long — range fighter — bomber, with additional 300 l fuel tanks under wings and an ETC 501 rack under the fuselage. Armament of only the 2 x MG 151/20 E. This version was developed into the series — produced **Fw 190G — 2**.

● **Fw 190A — 5/U9** — an experimental version with more armament: two 13 mm MG

131 instead of the MG 17 in the fuselage, another pair of MG 151/20 E in place of the MG FF in wings. Only two aircraft were built (W.Nr. 150812 and 150816), one of which (BH+CF, W.Nr. 150816) was subsequently used for testing of the more powerful BMW 801 versions (as the **V35** prototype).

● **Fw 190A — 5/U10** — an experimental version (two aircraft: W.Nr. 150861 and

Fw 190 A — 0/U4 which served for testing of external bomb armament, which led the way to developing armament sets for Fw 190 F. This is probably the W.Nr. 0008, KB+PD.

(MVT via M. Krzyżan)

Fw 190 A−0, W.Nr. 0010, the first aircraft powered by the BMW 801 C−1 engine.

(MVT via M. Krzyżan)

six MG 151/20 E cannon, including two WB 151/20 pods with two cannon each. Full armament comprised 2 x MG 17, 2 x MG 151/20E plus 2 x 2 MG 151/20E. This was the prototype of Rüstsatz 1 (R1) for the **Fw 190A**. Two aircraft were built: BH+CC, W.Nr. 150813 and BH+CD, W.Nr. 150814.

● **Fw 190A−5/U13** − three prototypes: the **V42**, W.Nr. 151083, GC+LA; V43, BH+CG, W.Nr. 150817 and **V44**, W.Nr. 150855. Long−range fighter−bomber with two underwing V. Fw Trg. (Verkleideter Focke−Wulf Träger) racks, capable of carrying both two 300 l tanks and 250 kg bombs. The flying equipment featured an auto−pilot. Leading−edge cutters against barrage balloons were planned. One of the prototypes (GC+LA) was temporarily fitted with cassette−type exhaust−glare dampers. Armament consisted of just two MG 151/20 E in the wing roots. The type was subsequently manufactured as the **Fw 190G−3**.

● **Fw 190A−5/U14** − torpedo aircraft, able to carry a single LT F5b air−launched torpedo on an under−fuselage ETC 502 rack. Enlarged (wider) fin (similar to the **Ta 152**) and a longer tailwheel leg to provide ground clearance for the torpedo. Armament − only two MG 151/20E. Two aircraft were tested: TD+SI, W.Nr. 150871 and TD+SJ, W.Nr. 150872.

● **Fw 190A−5/U15** − trials aircraft (VL+FG, W.Nr. 151282) modified to carry the **Blohm und Voss 246** *Hagelkorn* (LT 950) − an unpowered radio−guided anti−ship flying bomb, with Askania ALSK 121 guidance unit. Extensive trials during late 1943. Subsequently W.Nr. 130975 an A−8/F−8 series aircraft, was also included in testing, but frequent failures of the **Bv 246**'s structure led to the abandonment of the trials.

● **Fw 190A−5/U16** − prototype of a fighter with heavier armament, to fight bomber formations. Instead of the MG FF, the heavier, 30 mm Rheinmetall−Borsig MK 108 cannon were installed in under−wing pods.

● **Fw 190A−5/U17** − fighter−bomber with an under−fuselage ETC 501 and four under−wing ETC 50 (4x50 kg bombs) racks. Together with the A−5/U−3 this was the prototype for the battle−field Fw 190F aircraft. The production variant was called **Fw 190 F−3/R1**. Armament − without the MG FF cannon. Existed also in tropical variant.

Because of the increased intensity of Allied bombing, the **Fw 190 A−5/R6** version, used by Reichsverteidigung (Reich Defence) units, was quite numerous.

It is also interesting to note here that there existed a variant of the **Fw 190 A−5** with external air intakes for the compressor. Cowlings with such intakes had been developed as an alternative solution, but were not used widely, mainly because of the increased aerodynamic drag. Moreover, a photograph is known of an **A−5** fighter in service with II./JG 54 on the Eastern Front, fitted provisionally for bombing duties by

150862) used for preparation of a wing suited to carry heavier armament, mainly the 20 and 30 mm cannon. Armament of 2 x MG 17 in the fuselage and 4 x MG 151/20 E was standardised for the A−6 version.

● **Fw 190A−5/U11** − an attack aeroplane with two 30 mm Rheinmetall−Borsig MK 103, fitted in underwing pods. Only one aircraft existed, RG+ZA, W.Nr. 151303. The installation was later standardised as the Rüstsatz 3 (R3).

● **Fw 190A−5/U12** − heavier armament of

Above: Fw 190 A−1, W.Nr. 067, TI+DQ. The aircraft was fitted with the FuG 25 IFF set.

Below: An Fw 190 A−2 in front of the factory hangar.

(Both MVT via M. Krzyżan)

An Fw 190 A−2 or A−3 with reduced armament, lacking MG FFs.

(MVT via M. Krzyżan)

fitting four (2 x 2) ETC 50 racks under the wings.

In the autumn of 1943 one **A−5**, W.Nr. 157347, was used as the prototype **V45** for tests of the GM 1 system which, by injection of N_2O (nitrous oxide) as an oxidising agent, enhanced the engine performance at high altitudes. This system was later standardised as the Rüstsatz 4 (R4).

In connection with the planned production start − up of BMW 801 F engines rated at 2,400 HP, intended to power the **A−9** and **A−10** versions, one **A−5**, W.Nr. 410230, was assigned (as the **V34** prototype) for trials with the experimental BMW 801 V85. However, there is no evidence that the engine was ever delivered and installed on the **Fw 190**. Series production of the BMW 801 F was never started, and the **A−9** aircraft received substitute TS/TU engines.

FOCKE−WULF 190 A−6

The basic change introduced in this version was to use MG 151/20 E cannon instead of the MG FF. To do this, the wing had to be modified to accept the heavier cannon and much larger ammunition bay. Extensive use was made during the trials of the **Fw 190A−5/U9** and **U10**. The set of strengthening elements and attachment points allowed production wings to accept mountings and ammunition bays for both 20 mm and 30 mm cannon, as well as under-wing armament pods, with the possibility of fitting an ammunition container inside. A suitable set of electric connections was also developed. Radio fit included the FuG 16 ZE as standard, with an additional circular antenna under the rear fuselage, for radio−navigation (some **A−5**s also received the latter modification). Series production was started in July 1943 and lasted until November, totalling 569 aircraft.

Standard armament of an **Fw 190 A−6** comprised 2 x MG 17 and 4 x MG 151/20E. Some aircraft featured ETC 501 racks, mainly to carry external fuel tanks (300 l), the modification not being identified by a separate designation. As opposed to the previous versions, the armament modifications were arranged in various Rüstsatz sets, including many new, not previously used:

● **Fw 190A−6/R1** — attack fighter with heavier armament of six cannon and two machine guns: 2 x MG 17, 2 x MG 151/20E + 2 sets of 2 MG 151/20 E in under−wing WB 151/20 E pods. This was based on the **A−5/U12** concept. In spite of the earlier plans, this variant was not widely used, and only a few **Fw 190 A−6/R1** reached Luftwaffe units, these including JG 11.
● **Fw 190A−6/R2** — anti−bomber interceptor, armed with 2 x MG 17, 2 x MG 151/20E and 2xMK 108; did not enter production.
● **Fw 190A−6/R3** — similar to the **A−5/U11**, armed with 2 x MG 17, 2 x MG 151/20E and 2xMK 103, not produced.
● **Fw 190A−6/R6** — standard armament plus W. Gr. 21 launchers.
● **Fw 190A−6/R2/R6** — an anti−bomber variant, with heavier armament and rocket launchers. Armed with 2 x MG 17, 2 x MG 151/20 E, 2 x MK 108 and 2 x W. Gr. 21. Only one prototype built, the V51, W.Nr. 530765.

● **Fw 190A−6/R7** — fighter with standard armament and extensive armouring, supplied to Reich Defence units. Often with 300 l tank on an ETC 501.

Above: An Fw 190 A−2 or A−3 (W.Nr. ...222), DN+CB. The aircraft's tailwheel has been damaged.

(MVT via M. Krzyżan)

Below: Fw 190 A−3, W.Nr. 447. The aircraft features an ETC 501 rack fitted with SC 50 bombs on an ER 4 adapter.

(MAP)

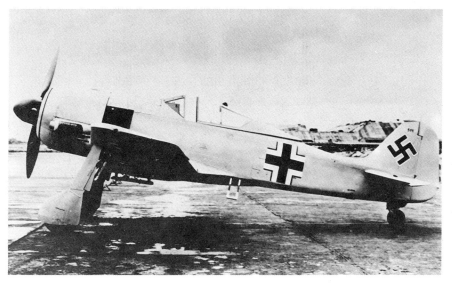

Fw 190 A—3, W.Nr. 511. The aircraft is fitted with dust filters and an ETC 501 rack.

(MVT via M. Krzyżan)

FOCKE—WULF 190 A—7

In November 1943 the **Fw 190 A—7** started to come off the production lines. This was developed from the A—5/U9 armament set, i. e. 2 x MG 131 and 4 x MG 151/20E. This gave birth to the characteristic elongated bulges on top of the fuselage in front of the cockpit, that housed the larger MG 131s. The Revi C/12D gunsight was replaced by the new Revi 16B. The stronger mainwheel hubs, used previously in the F version, were fitted as standard.

The aircraft were usually fitted with the ETC 501 rack for bombs or 300 l fuel tank, although some **Fw 190 A—7** were fitted with a smaller attachment that only accepted the fuel tank. Some also featured reduced armament (2 x MG 131 and 2 x MG 151/20E) which proves that these were intended for dogfighting Allied fighters. Apart from the basic **Fw 190 A—7**, three Rüstsatz sets were developed: R1. R2 and R6.

One A—7 (W.Nr. 380394) was used to test new, flattened, drop tanks called „Doppelreiter". Each of these could take 270 l of fuel, and they were fitted on top of the wing, thus hopefully achieving low drag and little reduction in top speed. The aircraft had its armament reduced to two MG 151/20E. Work on the tanks was carried out in the Forschungsanstalt Graf Zeppelin (FGZ) under M. Sc. (Eng.) Isemann. After a series of successful trials the RLM decided — to the great dismay of the designers — not to introduce the modification in order to keep production going smoothly!

In January 1944, after only 80 A—7s of all variants were built, the production was abandoned in favour of the more modern A—8.

FOCKE—WULF 190 A—8

The new variant differed mainly in equipment fitted. The most important modification consisted in installing the MW 50 system (water injection to temporarily increase power output), with the 118 litre cylindrical tank fitted in the rear fuselage. If necessary, this could also be used as an additional fuel tank. The tank caused the CoG to move aft, and to counteract that the under—fuselage ETC 501 rack was repositioned 20 cm forward. Starting from the A—8 the rack was fitted as standard on all aircraft. The FuG 16 ZY radio set was fitted which, apart from the additional circular radio—navigation aerial, also featured a *Morane*—type aerial under port wing. The Pitot tube was repositioned from mid—wing to wing—tip position, a give—away to distinguish an A—8 from an A—7.

Fw 190A—8, like the previous marks, could be fitted with various Rüstsatz sets (R1, R2, R3, R4, R6, R7, R8, R11, R12). However, the R1, R3 and R4 were abandoned, while the R2, R6, R7 and R8 were the most frequently used types. R11 and R12 night fighters were not numerous. They featured some equipment modifications, for example the MG 131 barrel ports were fitted with flash hiders, some aircraft

- **Fw 190A—6/R8** — a Rüstsatz combining the R2 (MK 108) and R7 (armouring). Often without the fuselage machine guns. Effective against American bomber formations.
- **Fw 190A—6/R11** — bad weather/night fighter. Anti—glare panels, landing light, PKS 12 auto—pilot and heated windscreen. Some aircraft were equipped with FuG 217 *Neptun* J—2 radar. Usually fitted with external fuel tank on an ETC 501 rack.

- **Fw 190A—6/R12** — a Rüstsatz combining the R2 and R11.

Apart from the above mentioned variants, one or two **Fw 190 A—6s** were fitted for trials with the more powerful BMW 801 TS, driving a three—blade VDM propeller with large wooden blades. The aircraft, coded VO+LY, featured additional oil cooler and tank armouring, and its armament was reduced to two MG 151/20 E in wing roots.

Above: Fw 190 A—5/U11, W.Nr. 151303, RG+ZA — template for the Rüstsatz 3.

(MVT via M. Krzyżan)

Below: Fw 190 A—5/U2, N?+WR.

(MAP)

were powered with more powerful BMW 801 TU engines, in some cases the FuG 125 *Hermine* radio—navigation set was installed, and the radar versions were most often equipped with the FuG 218 *Neptun* J—3.

Apart from the variants listed above, the **A—8**s/**F—8**s were often used for trials of experimental armament and equipment sets, as well as power plants. Unfortunately, only a small portion of the relevant documents have survived, so it is not possible to describe all modifications, nor to clarify some contradictory information. The following armament sets are known, however:

● SG 116 *Zellendusche* — a 3—barrel battery based on MK 103 cannon in the rear fuselage, triggered by a photo—cell;

● SG 117 *Zellendusche* — a 6—barrel battery of the above—mentioned installation;

● Rohrblock 108 — a similar, 7—barrel battery of MK 108 cannon elements, photo—cell triggered. Most probably those were just barrels, armed with a single shell each. When the first one fired, the others were triggered automatically by the recoil force. This anti—bomber armament type was tested on the **Fw 190 A—8**, W.Nr. 733713 which was designated as the **V74** prototype;

● SG ...? *Harfe* — a set of 3—4 15—tube 20 mm rocket launchers, installed in the rear fuselage and on its sides. At least one prototype so fitted was shown to General Adolf Galland;

● Ruhrstahl X—4 (**Ru 344**) — wire—guided rocket missiles, launched from under—wing racks, most probably the ETC 503. The armament was developed to attack ground targets (tanks) as well as bombers (with different warheads). **F—8** aircraft were used for trials.

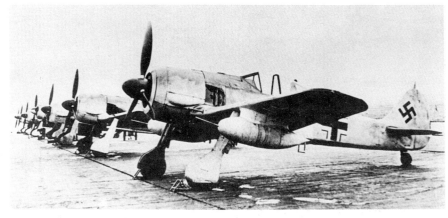

Above: A line—up of Fw 190s. The aircraft in the foreground is an Fw 190 A—4/U8 (G—1). *(MAP)*

Below: An Fw 190 A—3/U7. Note the supercharger external air intakes.

(MVT via M.Krzyżan)

From 1944 the fighter production was developed (the so called Jägernotprogramm — Emergency Fighter Programme) which necessitated further co—ordination of production and co—operation. Thus, the **Fw 190 A—8** was mass—produced in almost every Focke—Wulf factory, including also the Cottbus, Sorau and Posen (Poznan,

An Fw 190 A—4/R6 — W. Gr. 21 missile launchers are well visible under wings.

(MAP)

Poland) works. Licence production was also started in NDW (Norddeutsche Dornier Werke) at Wismar. Smaller factories were responsible for overhauls and re — assembly of aircraft withdrawn from front — line units, and small parts manufacture. Special co — ordination committees took care of effective operation of the system and continuous deliveries. No less than 1,334 **A — 8**s were built.

FOCKE — WULF 190 A — 9

The next version, and the last of all the As was the **Fw 190 A — 9**. At first, this was supposed to be powered with the 2,400 HP BMW 801 F. However, BMW failed to start production in time, consequently the 2,000 HP BMW 801 S, with a more effective, 14 — blade fan, was used instead. The engines were delivered as complete BMW 801 TS power plants, since they required a more effective oil cooler and a larger oil tank. These were installed next to each other, in the form of a ring, in front of the engine, under an armoured cover, the thickness of the armour being increased from 6 mm to 10 mm. It was planned to use as standard a three — blade constant — speed airscrew with wooden, large — chord blades. However, for unknown reasons, many **A — 9**s (unlike the **F — 9**s) were fitted with the metal VDM 9 — 12176 A propellers from the previous variant.

The **A — 9** airframe differed from the **A — 8** only in an enlarged cockpit hood, adapted from the **Fw 190 F — 8**, although some aircraft also received a new tail section with the broader fin of the **Ta 152**. The armament and Rüstsatz sets were the same as in **A — 8**, but in many cases the MG 151/20 Es in outer wings were removed.

Production started in late autumn 1944 and continued in parallel with **A — 8**s, monthly output depending on the availability of BMW 801 TS power plants.

A much modified project, the **Fw 190 A — 10**, powered with the BMW 801 F, was also developed, but was never built because of the war situation.

FOCKE — WULF 190 S

In connection with the reorganisation of dive — bomber into fighter — bomber units and the need to convert **Ju 87** pilots to Fw

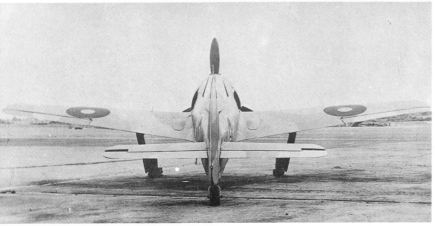

190s, thc Luftwaffe placed an order for a two—seat training version.

The modification was carried out in the spring of 1944, based on the **A—8** airframe, which received the additional designation of U1. The second cockpit was placed immediately aft of the front one, replacing the tank of the MW 50 system, not used in this model. The rear cockpit hood was modified to a three—piece, side—opened version (similar to the **Bf 109 G—12**), with a duralumin aft fairing on top of the rear fuselage. Three aircraft were modified, to become the template for combat fighter conversions. These were usually damaged aircraft withdrawn for repairs, so the exact number of two—seater Fw 190s is difficult to establish, but they were not very numerous.

They were based on **A—5**s and **A—8**s and designated **S—5** and **S—8**, respectively (S=Schulflugzeug — training aircraft).

NC 900

This designation was given to 64 **Fw 190**s, mainly **A—5**s and **A—8**s, assembled at the French SNCAC works from parts and sub-assemblies left in a repair and overhaul facility at Auxerre, and captured by the Allies. The aircraft were used in the Armee de l'Air (French Air Force).

FOCKE—WULF 190 F

Extremely promising results of the fighter Fw 190 As led the RLM to consider other uses for the aircraft. Greatest expectations were raised by the possible fighter—bomber role in which the **Fw 190** could replace the obsolete **Henschel 123** biplanes, and partly also the **Junkers 87** dive—bombers, even though the latter (continuously modified) were still quite effective, especially in the Eastern Front.

Above: An early Fw 190 A—5/U8, with V. Tr.—Ju 87 racks instead of V.Mtt—Schloß. The variant was produced as Fw 190 G—2, but with later type racks.

Right: Fw 190 A—5, W.Nr. 151163, BG+KC at a factory airfield.

(Both: MVT via M.Krzyżan)

Fw 190 A–7 with 'Doppelreiter' system tanks.   *(Both: MVT via M. Krzyżan)*

Thus, as early as 1942, the RLM developed the **Fw 190** specification, to cover development of a dedicated battlefield support version (Schlachtflugzeug). A special design study of the Fw 190 airframe was carried out, called Ra 2 (Rechnerische Ankündigung 2) that covered various concepts of the **Fw 190 A** modification.

During May 1942 preliminary trials of a modified **Fw 190 A−0/U4**, W.Nr. 0008 were carried. The aircraft received ETC 50 racks for 50 kg bombs under fuselage and wings. The promising results encouraged further tests, during which the increased weight was found to be the main problem. This was caused both by the bomb load and by the need to add protective armour against ground fire. The armour consisted of plates covering the bottom fuselage near the fuel tanks, lower engine cowling and landing gear covers. The cockpit side armouring, planned at the beginning was finally abandoned due to excessive weight. This was also the reason why new, stronger undercarriage legs were not introduced. In-

Above: Fw 190 S−5, W.Nr. 410011, GO+MV.

(MVT via M. Krzyżan)

Right: Fw 190 S−5 student cockpit.

(MVT via M. Krzyżan)

Below and below right: Fw 190 S instructor cockpits. Note the different arrangement of controls on the panels, depending on the time of conversion and works which carried it out.

(MVT via M. Krzyżan)

Another view of the Fw 190 S−5, W.Nr. 440011, GO+MV.

(MVT via M. Krzyżan)

stead, the air pressure in the shock absorbers was increased.

Following start−up of the **Fw 190 A** fighter mass production, the attack version development continued, using **A−3, A−4**, and **A−5** airframes which, after introduction of the type in Luftwaffe units, proved quite suitable for this role. However, the

Below: Cockpit cover of the two−seater Fw 190 S−8, W.Nr. 584219. Note that the markings and side no. are fictitious.

(J.Wróbel)

Below right: Forward fuselage of the Fw 190 S−8, W.Nr. 584219, at the RAF Museum, Hendon. Note the open cooling ports in the rear engine cowling. The JG 54 emblem has been applied in the post−war period.

(J.Wróbel)

Below: Two−seater training Fw 190 S−8, an aircraft with a flat rear cockpit canopy. Note the way of cockpit cover opening.

(via A. Price)

19

Fw 190 A—6, BH+...? at a factory airfield.

(MVT via Krzyżan)

increased weight of the external armament and equipment required trading some of the internal weapons, namely two of the wing—mounted MG FF cannon, to ensure retention of a decent flying performance with the increased weight.

FOCKE—WULF 190 F—1 and F—2

Fw 190 A—4/U3 with reduced armament (2 x MG 17 in the fuselage + 2 x MG 151/20 E in wings), fitted with an under—fuselage ETC 501 bomb rack (able to carry a single 250 kg or 500 kg bomb, or four 50 kg bombs on an ER 4 adapter), was found to be the optimum attack aircraft. The RLM ordered 30 of these, but only 18 were built, as the A—4 was replaced by the A—5 in the meantime. This was modified for fighter—bomber duties as well. The most numerous of several versions was the Fw 190 A—5/U3 (equipped similarly to the A—4/U3) of which 63 were built. Some of these also received tropical accessories (A—5/U3/trop).

Favourable opinions coming from Luftwaffe units, as well as the ever increasing need for fighter—bomber aircraft, led to the decision at the Focke—Wulf works to

Fw 190 A—8/R11 with FuG 217 *Neptun* J—2 radar. The aircraft carries reduced armament and lightweight attachment for a fuel tank. Armourers' access to the top fuselage weapon bay was limited due to rod aerials fitted to the cover which prevented the latter from full opening.

(MVT via Krzyżan)

Below: The experimental Fw 190 A—6, VO+LY, used for trials of the more powerful engine.

(MAP)

Fw 190 A – 2, 7./JG 2, France, 1942

Fw 190 A – 5, unknown unit, Eastern Front

Fw 190 A – 4, W.Nr. 142310, 2./JG 54, Uffz. Helmut Brandt, northern part of the Eastern Front, January 1943

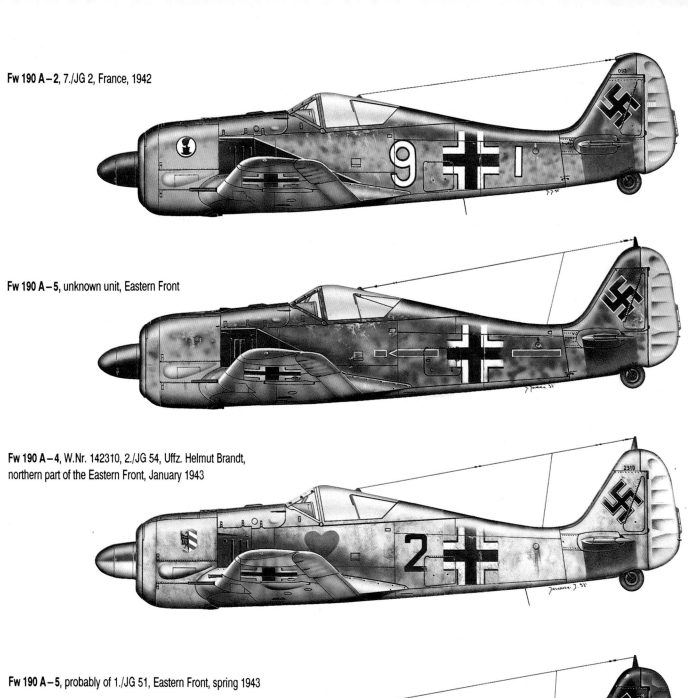

Fw 190 A – 5, probably of 1./JG 51, Eastern Front, spring 1943

Fw 190 A – 6/R11 with FuG 217 Neptun radar, 2./NJGr 10, Germany, 1944

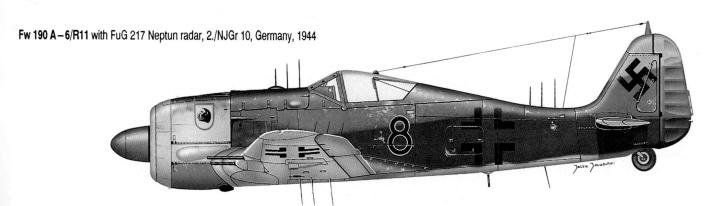

Fw 190 A–8 with another 'Doppelreiter' system fuel tanks.

(MVT via M. Krzyżan)

including some **F–2 trop** tropicalised aircraft.

FOCKE–WULF 190 F–3

Other **A–5**–based modifications were also included into the **Fw 190F** line. These were the **Fw 190 A–5/U10, A–5/U11, A–5/U12** and **A–5/U17**. The latter became the template for a new variant called **Fw 190F–3**, introduced into production in May 1943.

The main production sub–variant, called **F–3/R1**, featured four (2 x 2) under–wing ETC 50 racks and a single under–fuselage ETC 501 suited for either bomb carriage or a 300 l drop fuel tank. Numerous aircraft of this version were delivered with tropical equipment (**F–3/R1/trop**). The **Fw 190 F–3/R3** with two 30 mm MK 103 cannon was supposed to follow on production lines, but it was abandoned following unsuccessful results of testing of the similarly armed **Fw 190 A–5/U11**, W.Nr. 151303, which showed poor manoeuvrability. Moreover, it was found that the MK 103 ammunition failed to penetrate Soviet T–34 tank armour. Only three **Fw 190 F–3/R3** were built, armed with two MK 103, albeit with somewhat different mountings and fairings.

The **A–5/U10** wing (also used in the **A–6** and later models) was also adopted for the F series. The **Fw 190 A–5/U12** armed with six 20 mm MG 151/20 E cannon was capable of destroying only poorly armoured ground targets, so development of this version in the F family was abandoned.

Production of **Fw 190 F–3** continued at Arado works in Warnemünde until April 1944 and totalled 247 aircraft of all variants. They were powered, like the fighter, with BMW 801 D–2 engines, rated at 1,730 HP.

The **Fw 190 F–4**, planned for October of 1943, differed from the **F–3** only in an improved electrical bomb–drop system. Again, two weapon sets were used: R1 (2 x 2 ETC 50 + ETC 501) and R3 (2 x MK 103), while the internal weapons were to remain unchanged (2 x MG 17 + 2 x MG

start assembly of an attack variant, designated the **Fw 190 F**, as an entirely new series, rather than just a modification of the fighter.

The first production series, the **Fw 190 F–1** was supposed to be based on the **Fw 190 A–5/U3**. The decision was taken, however, to include the **Fw 190 A–4/U3** among the F variants, so this version was called the **F–1**, while the **Fw 190 A–5/U3** received the designation of the **F–2**. In all, a total of 271 **Fw 190 F–2** were built by May 1943,

Above: Fw 190 A–8 with 'Doppelreiter' system fuel tanks — port view.

Below: Heading-on view of the Fw 190 A–8 with additional fuel tanks on the leading edge of wings.

Below right: Front view of the port wing fuel tank.

(All photos: MVT via M. Krzyżan)

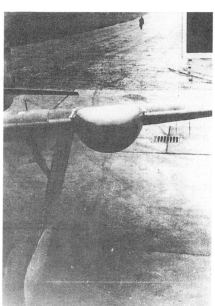

Fw 190 F—1 with an ER 4 adapter on an ETC 501 rack.

(MVT via Krzyżan)

151/20 E). None entered production, however.

Similarly, the two subsequent variants, the **Fw 190 F—5** and **F—6**, were not produced. They would have been powered by the new BMW 801 F engines, rated at 2,400 HP, tested on the prototypes **Fw 190 V36** (**F—5**), and **Fw 190 V37** and **V40** (**F—6**). Since BMW failed to start production of the engines, both variants were cancelled. A similar fate befell the **Fw 190 F—7**, based on the **A—7**, when the decision was taken to concentrate on the much improved Fw 190 **A—8** (in late 1943) also the **F—7** series was abandoned.

FOCKE—WULF 190 F—8

This **A—8**-based variant was the built in larger numbers than any other F version. Assembly was started at the Warnemnde Arado works in March 1944, and at the NDW—Wismar works in April.

The BMW 801 D—2 power plant was used, only in the C3 (96 octane) fuel version, fitted with additional fuel injection at the supercharger port inlet to enable temporary (10—15 minutes) boosting of the engine at altitudes below 1,000 m. Most equipment was identical to the Fw 190 **A—8**, although the FuG 16 ZY radio set was replaced (since April 1944) by the FuG 16 ZS which allowed direct communication with ground troops on the battlefield. Only few aircraft (as opposed to earlier variants) received tropical equipment with dust filter. One of the more visible modifications in the **F—8** model was the new, wider, rear cockpit canopy, introduced in late 1944. It improved side—forward view from the cockpit, especially important in a fighter—bomber. The armament consisted of two 13 mm MG 131 machine guns in the fuselage and two MG 151/20 E cannon in wings.

Many **F—8** aircraft of the first production series featured additional armouring as fitted to **F—3**s, but in order to reduce weight and improve performance this was abandoned, leaving only the standard Fw 190 **A—8** armouring. Since the **A—8** fighters were fitted with ETC 501 racks as standard, these were also mounted on all **F—8**s, but without the drop tank stabilisers.

With the beginning of 1944, because of the difficult situation in the Eastern Front, the Luftwaffe needed desperately an attack plane able to destroy armoured vehicles, including heavy tanks with very thick armour. This necessitated arming the **Fw 190 F** with weapons other than bombs. The task was not an easy one, since the Luftwaffe did not have any proven weapon system of this kind capable of being fitted on small, fighter aircraft. The only way led through trial—and—error search of a proper armament.

The first to be tested were the 280 mm W.Gr. 28/32 surface—surface missiles with a very powerful warhead. These proved useless, however, since their curved and un-

stable flight—path rendered precise aiming impossible. Then the Panzerschreck 1 rocket launchers were tested, in sets of three and attached under wings on ETC 50 or ETC 71 racks. Each launcher was armed with cumulative warhead missiles. They were replaced by more modern Panzerschreck 2

(PD 8.8) in four sets of two. The warload consisted of 88 mm rockets with cumulative warheads, fired individually or in salvos. So armed **Fw 190 F—8/trop**, W.Nr. 580383, CM+WL, was tested by Major Eggers at Udetfeld. The results were quite satisfactory, even though the range was still too

Fw 190 F—3/R1/tp. KO+MD, with ETC 50 racks.

(MAP)

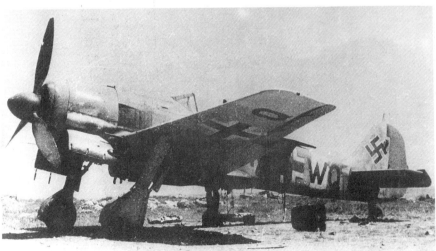

An abandoned Fw 190 F—8/R1.

(MVT via Krzyżan)

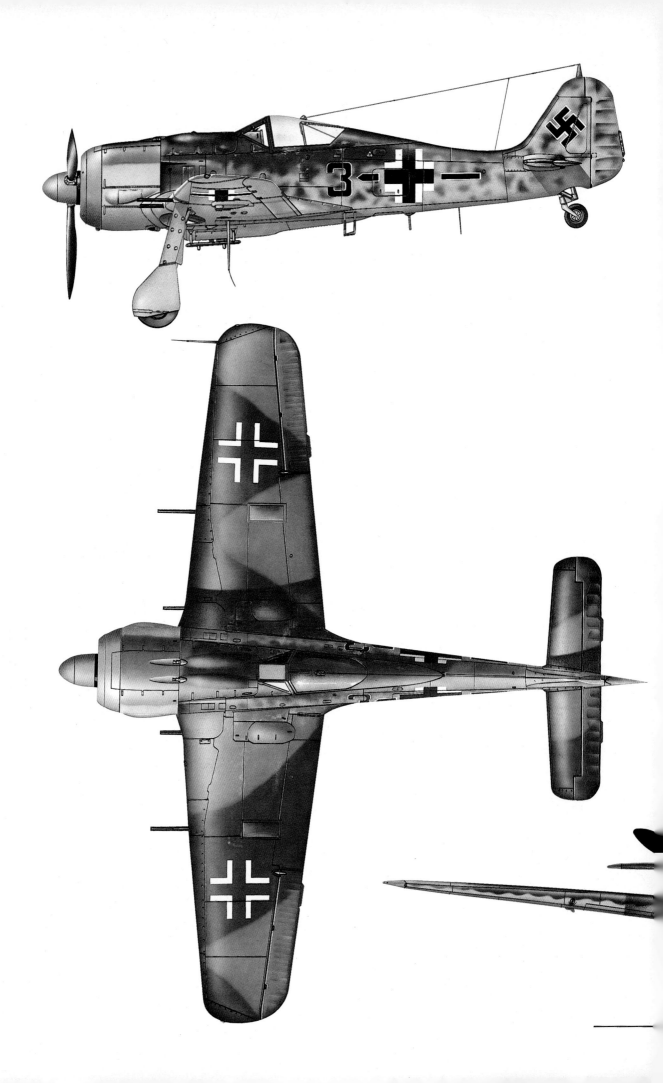

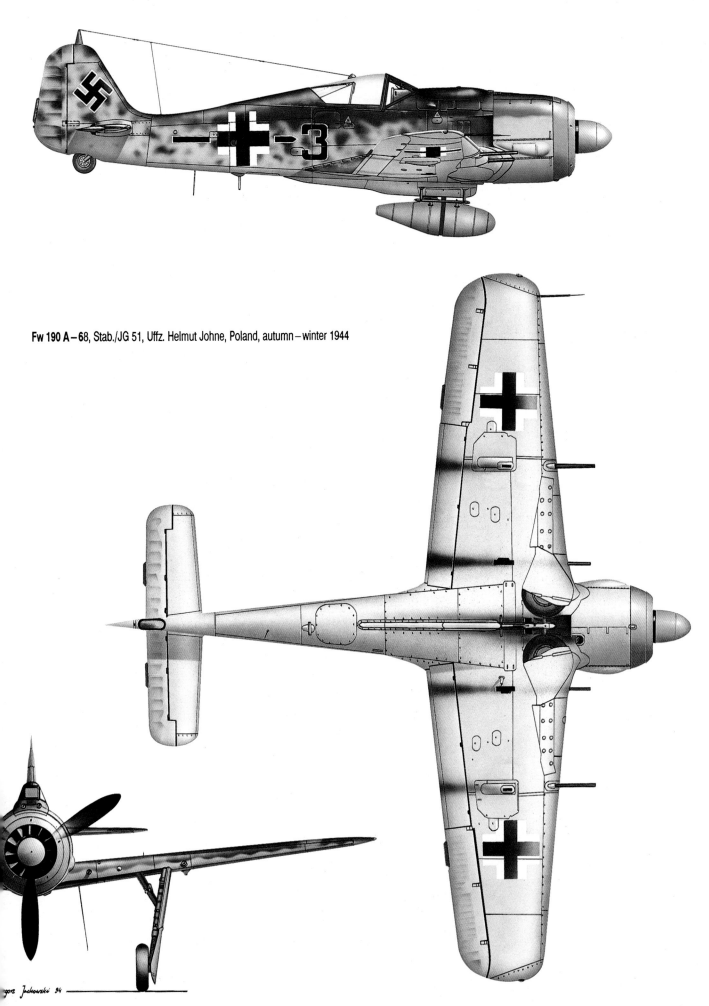

Fw 190 A – 68, Stab./JG 51, Uffz. Helmut Johne, Poland, autumn – winter 1944

orgorz Jackowski 94

Fw 190 F — 8/trop, W.Nr. 580383, CM+WL. This aircraft was used for trials of various external weapon arrangements, including ETC 503 and ETC 71 under wings and ER 4 adapter on the under — fuselage ETC 501.

(MAP)

short (137 m) and the aiming rather poor. In spite of that, in October 1944, a small number of **Fw 190 F — 8**s with Panzerschreck 2s entered service on the Eastern Front.

December 1944 saw the introduction of much more effective Panzerblitz 1 (Pb 1) rocket sets, consisting of six or, more often, eight R4M air — to — air missiles, modified for anti — tank duties by fitting 80 mm M8 warhead, capable of destroying armour 90 mm thick. With the Pb 1 it was possible to destroy tanks from the maximum distance of 200 m. The only limitation was the maximum speed of 490 km/h, not to be exceeded when firing the missiles (in pairs or in two salvos of 8). Until February 1945 the Luftwaffe received 115 **Fw 190 F — 8/Pb 1**s.

The Pb 1 was followed by the Panzerblitz 2 (Pb 2) which differed in that the M8 warhead was replaced with a cumulative charge, able to penetrate through 180 mm thick armour. Another set, called Panzerblitz 3 (Pb 3), was also developed by fitting 210 mm cumulative warheads, but this failed to be used operationally before the end of hostilities. Similar was the fate of the Abschußgerät 140 (AG 140) which was made up of two 210 mm missile launchers of different type than in the Pb 3. The AG 140 trials were carried out on three **Fw 190 F — 8**s, designated as prototypes: **V78**, W.Nr. 551103; **V79**, W.Nr. 583303; and **V80**, W.Nr. 586600.

Apart from the rocket installations described above, **Fw 190 F — 8**s were also used for testing other experimental air — to — ground weapon systems, such as Rheinmetall SG 113 A Förstersonde twinned launchers, fitted obliquely in wings and firing downwards. They were triggered automatically when the aircraft was overflying a tank (the Förster probe principle was used to detect magnetic field change). Three prototypes were prepared at the FGZ (Forschungsanstalt Graf Zeppelin): the **Fw 190 V75**, W.Nr. 582071 and the W.Nr. 586586 in October 1944, and the W.Nr. 933425 in December. However, the unit lacked precision and the project was abandoned.

In June 1944 a special Gero II flame — thrower was developed in three versions: A, B, and C, by the special group of Colonel Haupt (Versuchsgruppe Oberst Haupt), designed specially for destroying ground targets. In February 1945 modification work was started on several **Fw 190 F — 8** to prepare them for fitting the flame — thrower by attaching special lower fuselage protective covers. It is not known whether the project was ever completed.

F — 8 aircraft were also assigned for flying trials of Ruhrstahl X — 4 (**Ru 344**) wire — guided air — to — air missiles. Their warheads were probably changed, to enable use against ground targets. The prototypes **Fw 190 V69**, W.Nr. 582072; **V70**, W.Nr. 580029, and three **F — 8** aircraft: W.Nr. 583431, 583438, and 584221 were used in trials. The program also included other missiles: Ruhrstahl X — 7 (**Ru 347**) Rotkäppchen, and **Henschel 298**. Trails were also conducted of the **Bv 246** (LT 950) Hagelkorn engineless flying bombs. It is also probable that the **Fw 190 F** was also supposed to carry the SB 800 RS special bomb, also known as the Prismen Rollbombe „Kurt" 1 and 2, designed for dam — busting. The bomb was tested at Leba on the Baltic coast (now in Poland), but it is not clear whether an **Fw 190 F** was used for the tests.

Anti — shipping attacks were one of the Fw 190 F — 8 roles, the torpedo equipment being included in some of the Umrüstbausatz sets:

● **Fw 190 F — 8/U1** — long — range fighter —

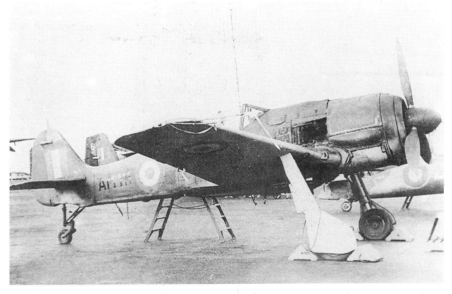

Above: Fw 190 F — 8/U3 (R15), tested by the RAF after the war.

Below: Fw 190 G — 3, W.Nr. 636 with V. Fw Trg. racks under wings.

(Both: MVT via Krzyżan)

bomber (supposed to replace the **Fw 190 G – 8** aircraft withdrawn from production), fitted with under – wing V.Mtt – Schloß (Verkleidetes Messerschmitt Schloß, from the **Bf 110**) together with additional fuel pumps inside the wing, to enable carrying two 300 l fuel tanks. Some aircraft featured ETC 503 racks instead of the fuel tank attachments, which enabled carrying two additional 250 kg bombs (in this case a fuel tank was carried on the under – fuselage ETC 501 rack). It was also possible to carry bombs on all racks (2 x 250 kg + 1 x 500 kg) thus limiting the range, but giving the ability to deliver 1,000 kg of bombs!

● **Fw 190 F – 8/U2** – torpedo – carrier with two under – wing ETC 503 racks or a single ETC 504 (or earlier ETC 501) under the fuselage. It also featured special TSA 2A (Tiefsturzanlage 2A) aiming system for precision launching of the BT – type (Bombentorpedo) air – launched torpedoes which enabled attacking marine targets at higher altitudes and at higher angles than the standard LT – type (Lufttorpedo) ones. Use of two BT 400 or a single BT 700 was planned. Only two MG 131 machine guns were carried. A small number of these aircraft was taken on charge by 11./KG 200.

● **Fw 190 F – 8/U3** – a torpedo – carrier specially modified to carry the BT 1400 heavy torpedo on an under – fuselage ETC 502 rack, specially developed at the TWP Gottenhafen – Hexengrund (Gdynia – Babie Doły in occupied Poland). A new, longer tailwheel unit was fitted to provide necessary clearance for the torpedo. The TSA 2A aiming device coupled with the FuG 101 radio – altimeter was used. The aircraft was fitted with a more powerful BMW 801 TS engine, rated at 2,000 HP. Also, the **Ta 152** tail unit was fitted.

Fw 190 A – 4/U8 with V. Tr. – Ju 87 racks with early – type duralumin fairings.
(MAP)

Fw 190 A – 5/U14, W.Nr. 150871, TD + SI, with an LT F 5B torpedo on a special ETC 502 rack.
(MAP)

● **Fw 190 F – 8/U4** – optimised for night operations, fitted with exhaust flame dampers on the BMW 801 TS engine. Standard equipment included PKS 12 auto – pilot, FuG 101 radio altimeter, TSA 2A, and other systems to facilitate night – flying. Bombs or torpedoes were attached on two under – wing ETC 503 racks. Only two MG 151/20E wing – mounted cannon were used. Probably only one aircraft was built (W.Nr. 586596). Even though NSGr 20 used many **Fw 190 F – 8**s with exhaust flame dampers, these were not the **F – 8/U4**, but standard aircraft modified in field, also **G – 8** or **F – 8/U1**.

● **Fw 190 F – 8/U5** – simplified version of the **F – 8/U2**, lacking some internal equipment.

When preparing production of the modified **Fw 190 F – 8**s (usually assigned to subcontractors and licence – manufacturers) it was decided to standardise almost all Umrüstbausatz modifications in the Rüstsatz range. Thus, the U variants were partly dubbed (in documents) as R modifications. Six variants are known, as follows:

● **Fw 190 F – 8/R1** – fighter – bomber with four under – wing ETC 50 racks for 50 kg bombs, later replaced with ETC 71 for 70 kg bombs (for example the AB 70 cassette bombs). Some aircraft featured both rack types (2 x ETC 50 + 2 x ETC 71) in pairs under each wing.

● **Fw 190 F – 8/R3** – an attack aircraft with two 30 mm MK 103 cannon; similar to the **A – 5/U11**, but with somewhat different mountings and fairings. Only two were built.

● **Fw 190 F – 8/R13** – optimised for night – fighting, similar to **F – 8/U4**.

● **Fw 190 F – 8/R14** – torpedo – carrier, capable of carrying the LT F 5b and LT 1B on ETC 502 rack, developed from the **Fw 190 A – 5/U14**. Fitted with the longer

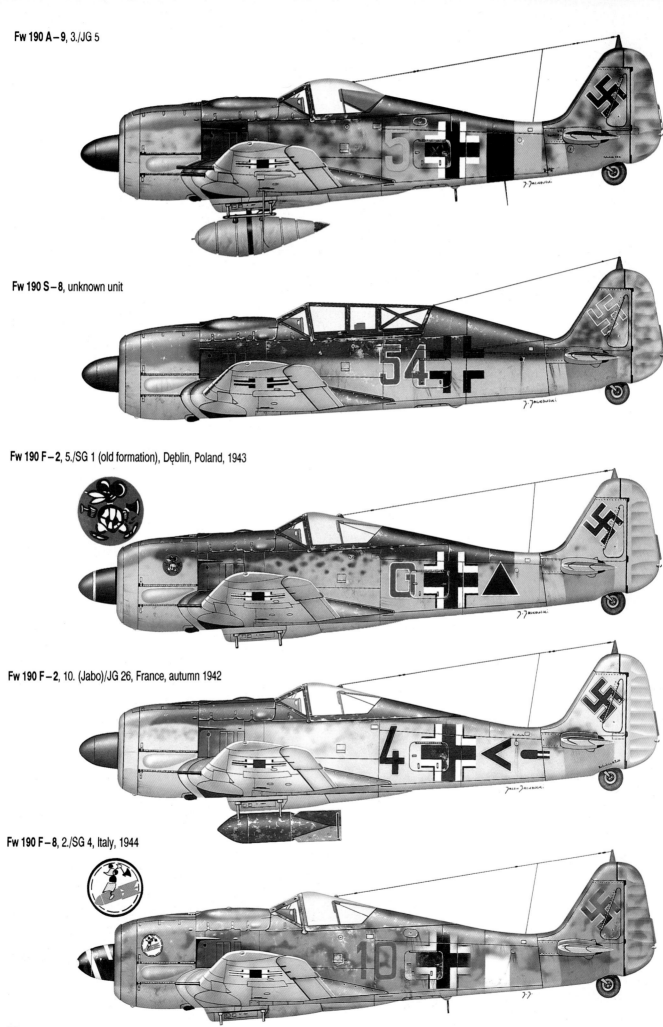

Fw 190 A – 9, 3./JG 5

Fw 190 S – 8, unknown unit

Fw 190 F – 2, 5./SG 1 (old formation), Dęblin, Poland, 1943

Fw 190 F – 2, 10. (Jabo)/JG 26, France, autumn 1942

Fw 190 F – 8, 2./SG 4, Italy, 1944

tailwheel leg and wider rudder of the **Ta 152**. Powered by the more powerful BMW 801 TS engine.

- **Fw 190 F − 8/R15** − similar to F − 8/U3.
- **Fw 190 F − 8/R16** − similar to F − 8/U2.

FOCKE − WULF 190 F − 9

In October 1944 a new version, the **Fw 190 F − 9**, entered production. It was developed from the **A − 9** fighter. The BMW 801 TS engine was driving a VDM 3.50 m diameter three − blade propeller with wooden Heine or Schwarz blades. All F − 9s featured the wider rear cockpit canopy. Some aircraft were also fitted with the **Ta 152** vertical tail. Internally mounted armament remained unchanged (2 x MG 131 + 2 x MG 151/20 E). The same set of R modifications was planned (with exception of the R3), but eventually only the standard and R1 versions were produced. A few aircraft were armed with Panzerblitz launchers.

At the turn of 1944, because of the critical situation in terms of strategic material supplies, and of the extensive fighter aircraft production programme, wooden substitutes for **Fw 190** components were deemed necessary. This applied mainly to the tail parts, flaps and ailerons; however, it is not known which of these, and in what numbers, were ever introduced. Small numbers of **Fw 190 F − 8** and **F − 9**, as well as **A − 8**, were used in *Mistel* composite aircraft.

The **Fw 190 F − 10**, based on the **Fw 190 A − 10**, was the next variant planned for production. This version was to be powered by a BMW 801 F (TF) engine and the **Ta 152** tail was planned as standard. New larger mainwheels of 740 x 210 mm were to be

Fw 190 G − 3, W.Nr. 160043, DP + ?.

(MVT via Krzyżan)

Fw 190 F − 8/R1 with ETC 71 racks under wings. The aircraft belonged to II. Gruppe of an unknown units, spring 1945.

(Philip Jarrett)

used. Because of the delay in deliveries of the BMW 801 F, no **F − 10** (just like the **A − 10**) was completed before the end of the war.

Fw 190 F − 15 was the next planned variant, differing from its predecessor in having the BMW 801 TS replacement engine. This project was derived from the prototype **Fw 190 V66**, W.Nr. 584002, but this was not (as some sources say) a direct prototype of the **F − 15**. **Fw 190 F − 16** was another project, and its prototype V67, W.Nr. 930516, was a converted **F − 8**. The only difference in comparison to the **F − 15** was replacing the FuG 16 ZE/ZS radio set with the FuG 15.

The last version, which did not even reach the prototype stage, was the **Fw 190 F − 17**, for anti − shipping duties, with the improved TSA 2D aiming system.

A total of approximately 7,000 Fw 190 F aircraft was built.

FOCKE − WULF 190 G

Almost in parallel with the production start − up of the attack **Fw 190 F**, developed for direct battlefield ground support (Schlachtflugzeug), another subtype derived from it entered production. This was a longer − range fighter − bomber Jabo − Rei (Jagdbomber mit vergrösserter Reichweite), designated **Fw 190 G**. This version was an attempt to create a fighter − bomber capable of carrying an air − to − ground warload further than 500 − 600 km behind the front − line, i.e. beyond the **Fw 190 F** combat radius.

Experimental Förstersonde installation on an Fw 190. This anti—tank weapon used tank's magnetic field to trigger the launcher which, although of 75 mm calibre, fired 45 mm rounds. To counteract the recoil force, another charge of similar weight was simultaneously fired upwards.

(via A. Price)

FOCKE—WULF 190 G—1

When developing the new version, the solutions of the **Fw 190 A—4/U8** long—range fighter—bomber were used extensively. The long range was achieved in that variant by using two under—wing drop fuel tanks for 300 l each, fitted on duralumin—faired Weserflug V. Tr. Ju 87 pylons.

The fuel weight increased to 880 kg led to performance reductions and longer take—off run, thus questioning the possibility of using smaller front—line airfields. It was necessary to reduce the weight by removing some armour or armament. The designers decided to do the latter, so the fuselage 7,9 mm MG 17 machine guns, and the outboard wing cannon were removed. The new **Fw 190 G—1** carried only two 20 mm MG 151/20 E cannon in wing roots with a reduced amount of ammunition (150 rounds per gun).

The under—fuselage ETC 501 rack could carry (as an offensive weapon) a 250 or 500 kg bomb, or four small 50 kg bombs

(on an ER 4 adapter). The radio equipment did not always include the FuG 25a IFF, also the radio direction finder was often removed. Because of the longer engine operation periods it was advisable to fit an additional oil tank in place of the fuselage MG 17 machine guns, under forward cowling in front of the canopy. A total of only some 50 **Fw 190 A—4/U8**, included in the **Fw 190 G** range and designated **Fw 190 G—1**, were manufactured. The under—wing attachment fairing was slightly enlarged and stiffened in production.

FOCKE—WULF 190 G—2

The new model, **Fw 190 G—2**, was derived from the modernised A—5 airframe, and its fighter—bomber U8 variant (**A—5/U8**), featuring the same set of modifications as the **A—4/U8**. Additional fuel (468 kg) was also carried in underwing tanks, but these (apart from a few early aircraft) were attached on simpler V.Mtt—Schloß racks and were dropped together with two side stabilisers. Moreover, the

duralumin fairings were abandoned, since they only reduced drag when the tanks were fitted, while after dropping them the drag rose leading to greater fuel consumption and a top speed lower by some 40 km/h. The new solution was more convenient in both configurations, and when flying without the tanks the smaller attachments only reduced the top speed by some 15 km/h. Similar to the G—1, some aircraft were fitted with an additional oil tank. Apart from the standard model, some aircraft were modified for night operations, being designated **Fw 190 G—2/N**. The main difference lay in exhaust flame dampers, to protect the pilot's eyes from the glare and reduce aircraft visibility for the enemy. Some aircraft received landing lights in the port wing leading edge.

FOCKE—WULF 190 G—3

In the summer of 1943 production of the modified **Fw 190 G—3** commenced. This series introduced the **Fw 190 A—6** wing as standard, and the under—wing fuel tank attachments were replaced with the V. Fw

Periscopic sight, sitted on Fw 190, used most probably for guiding the aircraft, equipped with SG116 and 117 Zellendusche, Rohrblock 108 or 'Förstersonde'.

(Both: MVT via M. Krzyżan)

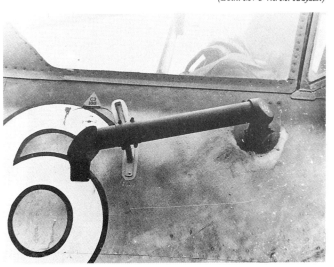

Trg. (Verkleideter Focke–Wulf Träger), similar to the ETC 501. They enabled the use of both fuel tanks and 250 kg bombs, which significantly increased the offensive capabilities of the aircraft. Apart from that, the **Fw 190 G–3** featured as standard the PKS 11 auto–pilot (sometimes the more modern PKS 12 was used) supposed to facilitate long–time flying (maximum endurance of the **Fw 190 G** was approx. 2.5 hours). Starting from October 1943 the **Fw 190 G–3** and subsequent variants were powered with BMW 801 D–2 engines fed with C3 (96 octane) fuel and fitted with additional fuel injection at the supercharger port inlet to enable temporary (10–15 minutes) boosting of the engine at low altitudes (below 1,000 m).

A tropical variant, called **Fw 190 G–3 trop**, was fitted with dustproof filter and other equipment for desert service.

A number of standard aircraft were modified by fitting equipment from the R sets for the G version:

● **Fw 190 G–3/R1** – heavily armed attack fighter with two WB 151/20 pods in place of the underwing V. Fw Trg. attachments. The armament consisted thus of two single MG 151/20 Es with 250 rounds per gun and two twinned MG 151/20 Es with 125 rounds per gun. The conversion was subcontracted in September 1943 to LZA works at the Luftwaffe base at Sagan–Köpper (now Żagań–Kopernia in Poland). No auto–pilot or additional armour was used. The aircraft were to be used against bombing raids as well as ground targets.

● **Fw 190 G–3/R5** – ground attack aircraft, converted according to the F–3/R1 standard. Instead of the V. Fw Trg. racks two ETC 50 racks were used (2 x 2 x 50 kg bombs). No additional armour or oil tank. Some aircraft were refitted with the fuselage MG 17 machine guns, and most retained the auto–pilot.

FOCKE–WULF 190 G–8

The next G version, and the last to reach production, was the **Fw 190 G–8**, based on the A–8 airframe. The G–4 through G–7 variants never reached beyond project status. The **G–8** incorporated all the modifications of the new fighter, plus the new larger cockpit canopy of the **Fw 190 F–8**. Some **G–8s** were prepared for night operations (**G–8/N**) by receiving the exhaust flame dampers. Even though no fuselage machine guns were fitted, the **G–8** received the modified bulged cowling forward of the windscreen, to accommodate MG 131. New ETC 503 racks were introduced under wings for bombs or fuel tanks. The following Rüstsatz sets were used on **Fw 190 G–8**:

● **Fw 190 G–8/R4** – never completed project with the GM 1 system to allow injection of nitrous oxide (N_2O) as oxidising agent, in order to enhance engine performance at high altitudes.

● **Fw 190 G–8/R5** – with four under–wing ETC 50 (or ETC 71) racks instead of two ETC 503s.

G–8 production continued from September 1943 until February 1944, when the **G–8** was abandoned in favour of the modified **F–8**. This was part of simplifying the production process as the last batch of **G–8** (February 1944) already lacked the auto–pilot. Thus an **Fw 190 G–8** (after installing the MG 131s) did not differ from the attack **Fw 190 F–8** (**G–8 = F–8/U1** with ETC 503s, and **G–8/R5 = F–8/R1**).

Individual **Fw 190 Gs** were provisionally modified to carry a heavy bomb under the fuselage (1,000; 1,600 or 1,800 kg). The modification consisted in strengthening the main undercarriage leg shock–absorbers and using wheels with more durable tyres. Also, the ETC 501 had to be replaced with special racks (Schloß 1000 or 2000). Such a heavily laden **Fw 190 G** required some 1,200–1,300 m for the take–off run.

A total of approximately 800 **Fw 190 G** of all sub–variants were manufactured. This was the last version of the **Fw 190** powered with a radial engine. It is worth noting here, that it is nearly impossible to establish the exact number of the **Fw 190s** produced. This results from several causes. First, manufacturing documentation of all the Focke–Wulf factories has not survived in full. Second, it is not known how many aircraft (especially the F variant) were manufactured in small specialised assembly works (Menibum, for example) that manufactured the torpedo–carrying and other special versions. Moreover, to make any precise listing even more complicated, overhaul and repair facilities often assembled 'recycled' aircraft from salvaged parts and subassemblies. For example a fuselage of one aircraft (which had its wings destroyed) could be married to wings of another. Such a 'kit' could well have a tail coming from yet another **Fw 190 A, F** or **G**. So assembled aircraft, often in a completely new variant, would receive a new factory number and would be delivered to a combat unit. The **Fw 190 F–8/R1** of the National Air Space Museum, Washington, DC (USA) is a good example here. When restoration work was started on the aircraft at Silver Hill, an old type plate was found inside

the fuselage with the W.Nr. (Werk Nummer – factory no.) 640069 which proved this came from an **A–7** airframe. However, after having been rebuilt during the war it was converted to an **Fw 190 F–8** and received a new factory no. (W.Nr. 931884) and introduced back into service.

The production total of **Fw 190s** with BMW 801 radial engines can be estimated at no less than 17,000 aircraft. Even though some sources quote very precise numbers, they are questioned by the very fact that they differ substantially between individual sources.

Off course the **Fw 190** development did not end with the A, F, and G version, but continued in the form of the liquid–cooled in–line engine–powered variants.

MISTEL

Like the **Bf 109** before, also the **Fw 190**, mainly in the **A–8/F–8/G–8** versions, were used as control aircraft for the bomber–assemblies known as *Mistel* (with unmanned **Ju 88s**) and *Mistel* S (training, with manned **Ju 88s**).

Various cumulative warheads were used in the **Ju 88** forward fuselage. Several versions of *Mistel* and *Mistel* S existed, differing in the **Ju 88** variant, as well as the control aircraft. **Fw 190s** were used in the *Mistel* 2, 3A, 3B, 3C, *Mistel* S2A, S3A, S3B, S3C. The **Fw 190s** used in *Mistel* composite sets had their armament removed, and an oil tank fitted in the gun bay in front of the cockpit (although many **Fw 190 G–8** already featured such a tank). Attachment points were fitted to the wing main spar and the rear fuselage, also electrical socket control systems were fitted there. A TSA 1 system was used for guidance. Because of the extent of modifications the *Mistel* **Fw 190s** received additional M designation, for example **Fw 190 A–8/M**.

There also existed a project of a *Mistel* set consisting of an **Fw 190** and a *Ta 154*.

The *Mistel* composite systems were developed by a centre at Nordhausen, and the **Ju 88** conversion involved participation from an overhaul centre at Leipzig–Mockau and ATG at Merseburg.

Several dozen *Mistels* of all types were built.

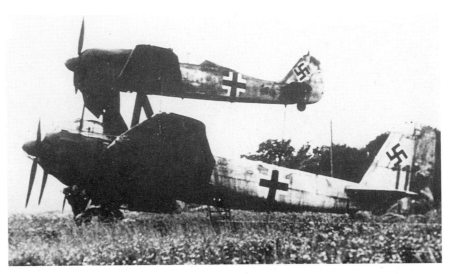

A training Mistel S2, composed of an Fw 190, probably an A–8, and a manned Ju 88G. Note lack of any codes or unit markings.

(MAP)

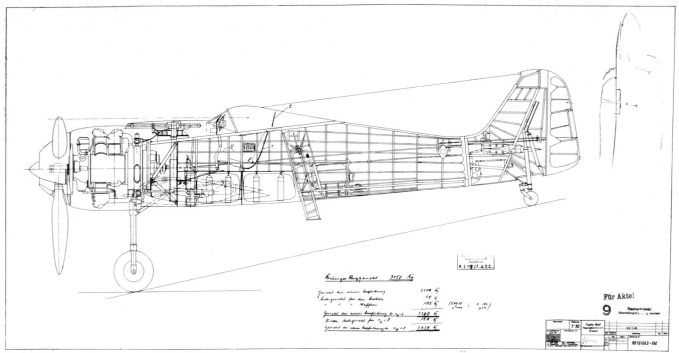

Above: Copy of a Focke-Wulf technical drawing
from July 1939 showing a variant of Fw 190 V1
development. The aircraft features longer forward
fuselage with fuselage-mounted armament and
mainwheel legs attached to fuselage framing. The
drawing carries hand-sketched seat/head-rest
armouring arrangement and weight calculations.
(M. Krzyżan collection)

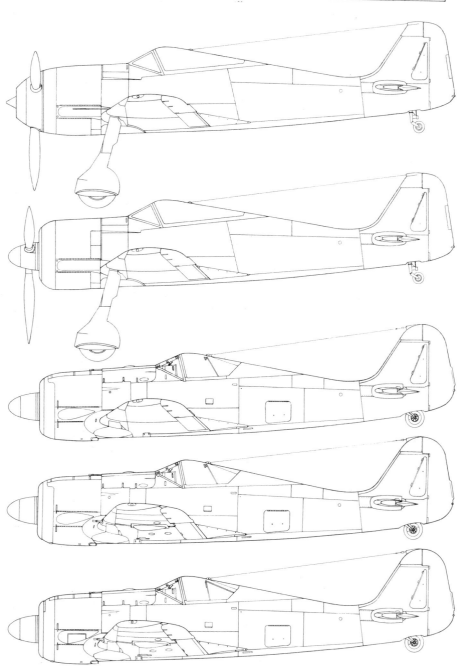

Fw 190 V1

Fw 190 V1 after modifications

Fw 190 V5k

Fw 190 A-0

Traced: **Adam Skupiewski**
Drawn: **Krzysztof Żurek**

Scale: 1:72

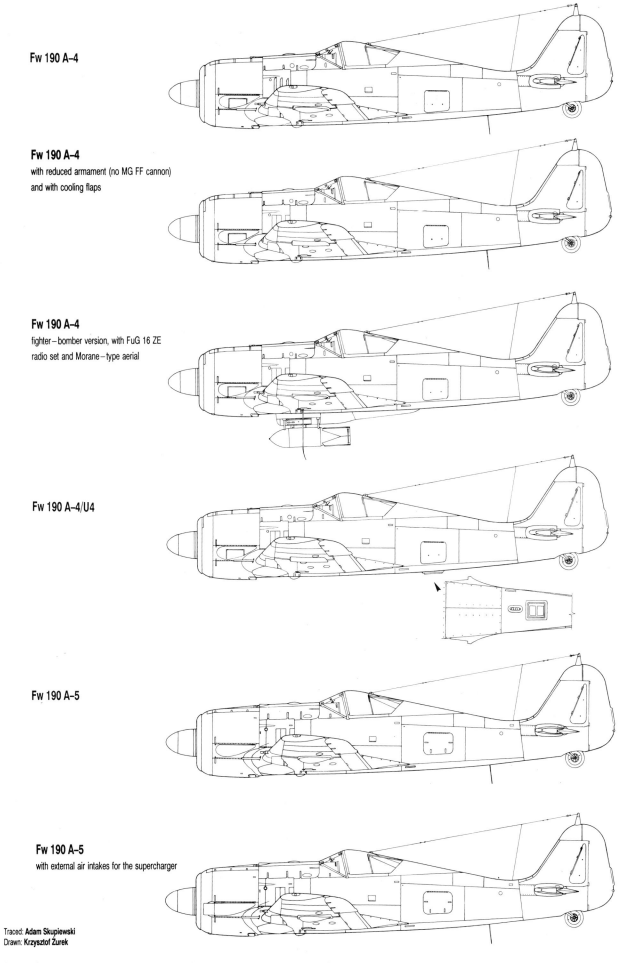

Fw 190 A–4

Fw 190 A–4
with reduced armament (no MG FF cannon)
and with cooling flaps

Fw 190 A–4
fighter – bomber version, with FuG 16 ZE
radio set and Morane – type aerial

Fw 190 A–4/U4

Fw 190 A–5

Fw 190 A–5
with external air intakes for the supercharger

Traced: **Adam Skupiewski**
Drawn: **Krzysztof Żurek**

Scale: 1:72

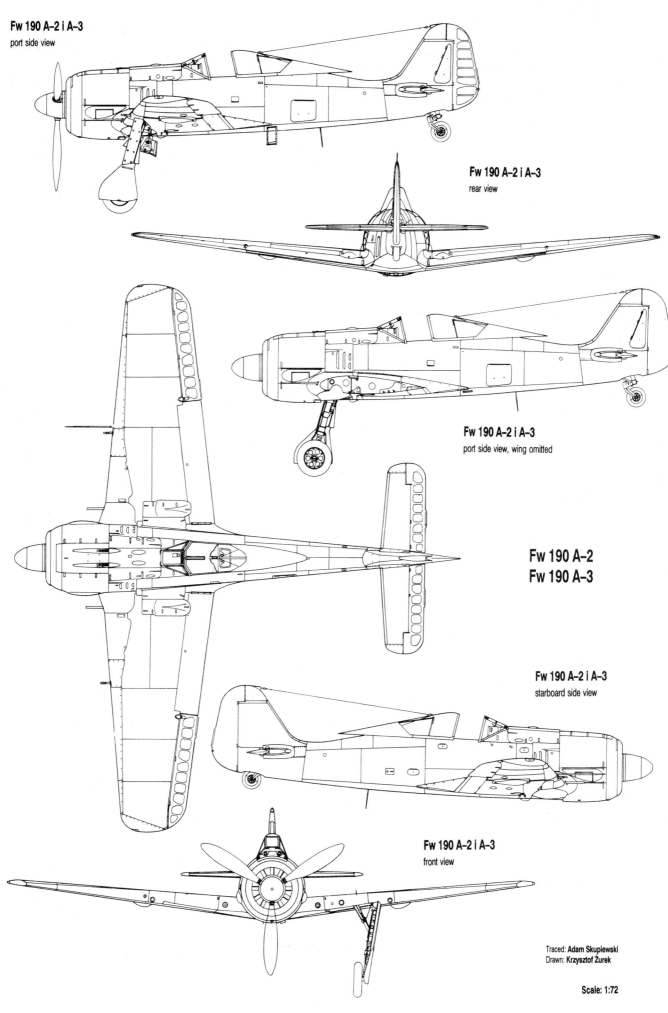

Fw 190 A–2 i A–3
port side view

Fw 190 A–2 i A–3
rear view

Fw 190 A–2 i A–3
port side view, wing omitted

Fw 190 A–2
Fw 190 A–3

Fw 190 A–2 i A–3
starboard side view

Fw 190 A–2 i A–3
front view

Traced: **Adam Skupiewski**
Drawn: **Krzysztof Żurek**

Scale: 1:72

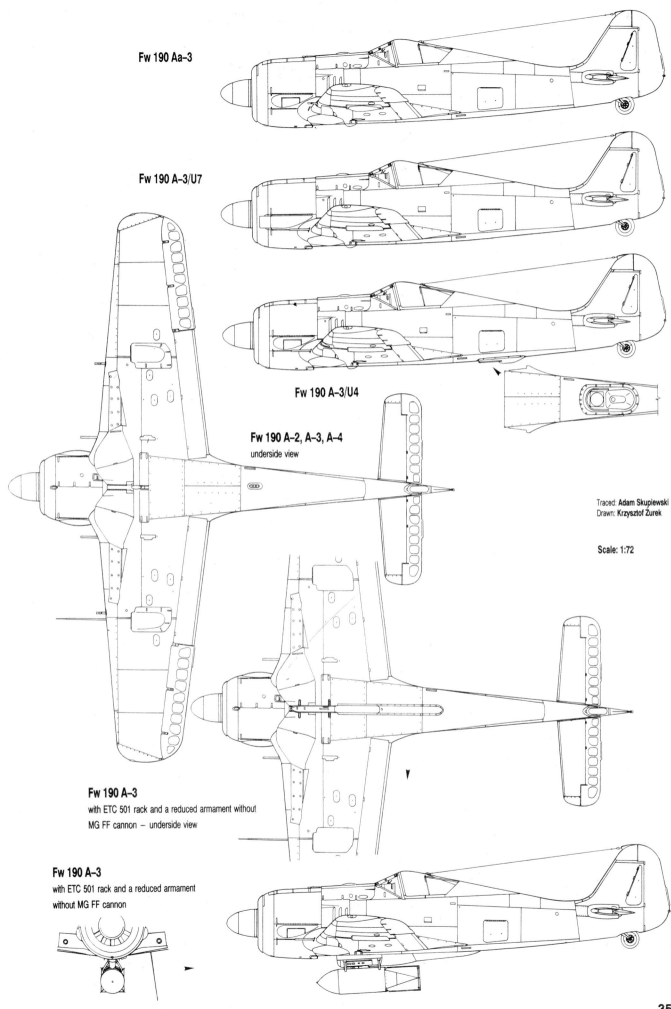

Fw 190 Aa-3

Fw 190 A-3/U7

Fw 190 A-3/U4

Fw 190 A-2, A-3, A-4
underside view

Traced: **Adam Skupiewski**
Drawn: **Krzysztof Żurek**

Scale: 1:72

Fw 190 A-3
with ETC 501 rack and a reduced armament without
MG FF cannon – underside view

Fw 190 A-3
with ETC 501 rack and a reduced armament
without MG FF cannon

Fw 190 A-5
with a reduced armament without MG FF cannon

Fw 190 A-5/U2

Fw 190 A-5/U11
pattern for Rüstsatz 3

Fw 190 A-5/U12
pattern for Rüstsatz 1

Fw 190 A-5/U14

Traced: **Adam Skupiewski**
Drawn: **Krzysztof Żurek**

Scale: 1:72

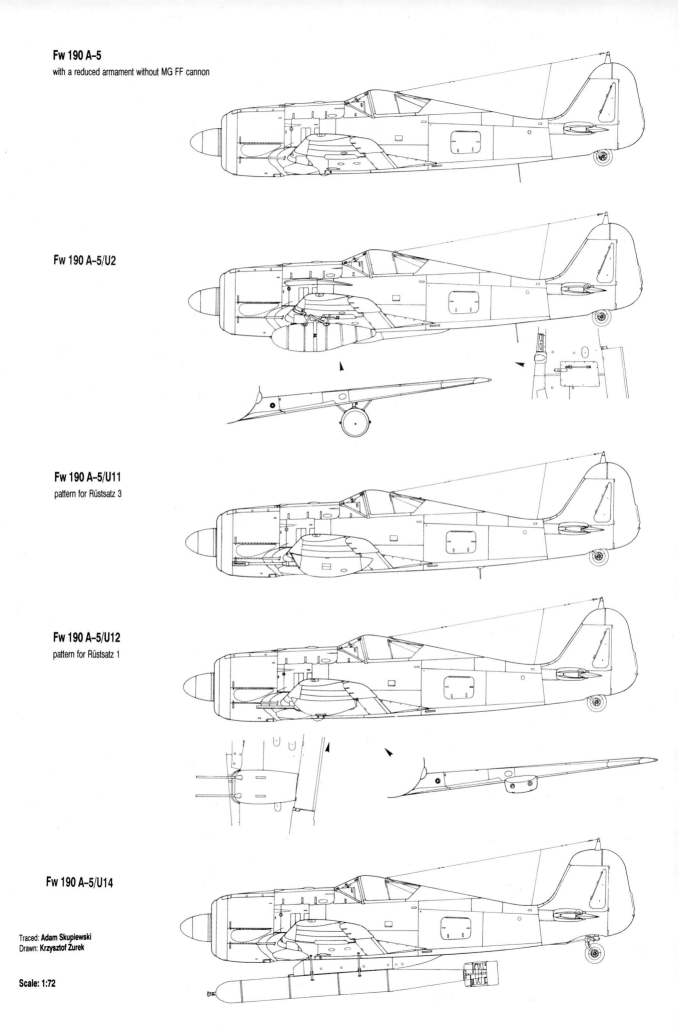

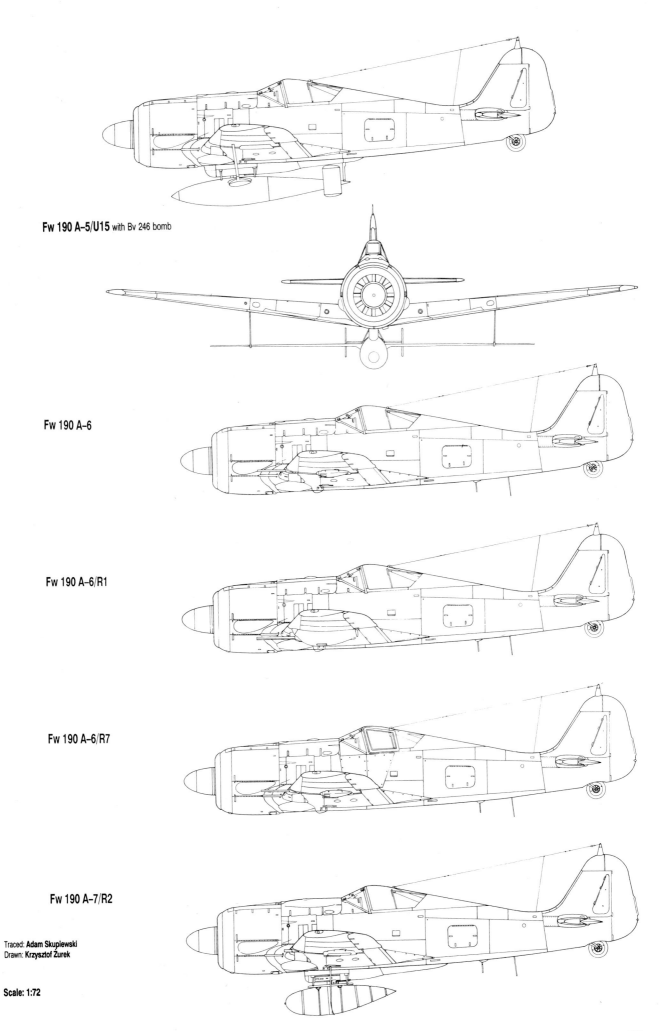

Fw 190 A–5/U15 with Bv 246 bomb

Fw 190 A-6

Fw 190 A-6/R1

Fw 190 A-6/R7

Fw 190 A-7/R2

Traced: **Adam Skupiewski**
Drawn: **Krzysztof Żurek**

Scale: 1:72

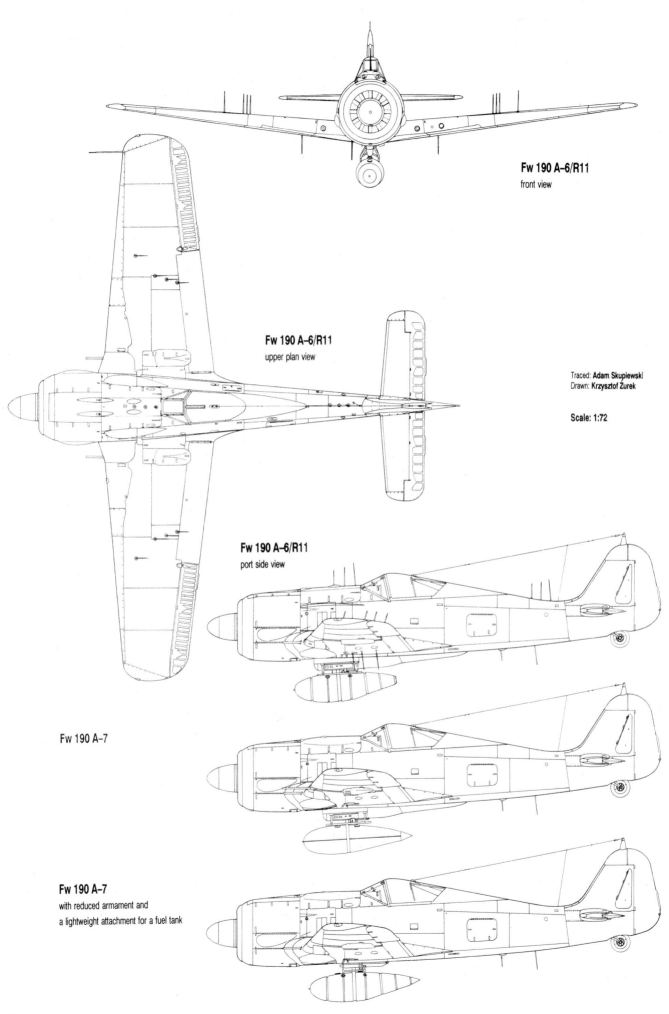

Fw 190 A–6/R11
front view

Fw 190 A–6/R11
upper plan view

Traced: **Adam Skupiewski**
Drawn: **Krzysztof Żurek**

Scale: 1:72

Fw 190 A–6/R11
port side view

Fw 190 A–7

Fw 190 A–7
with reduced armament and
a lightweight attachment for a fuel tank

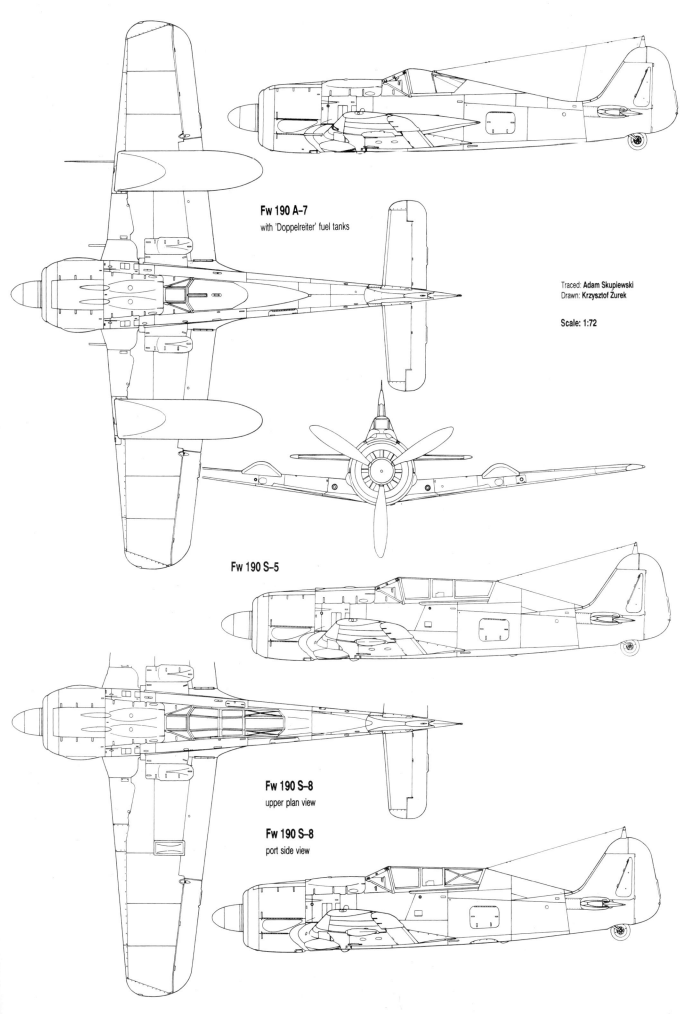

Fw 190 A-7
with 'Doppelreiter' fuel tanks

Traced: **Adam Skupiewski**
Drawn: **Krzysztof Żurek**

Scale: **1:72**

Fw 190 S-5

Fw 190 S-8
upper plan view

Fw 190 S-8
port side view

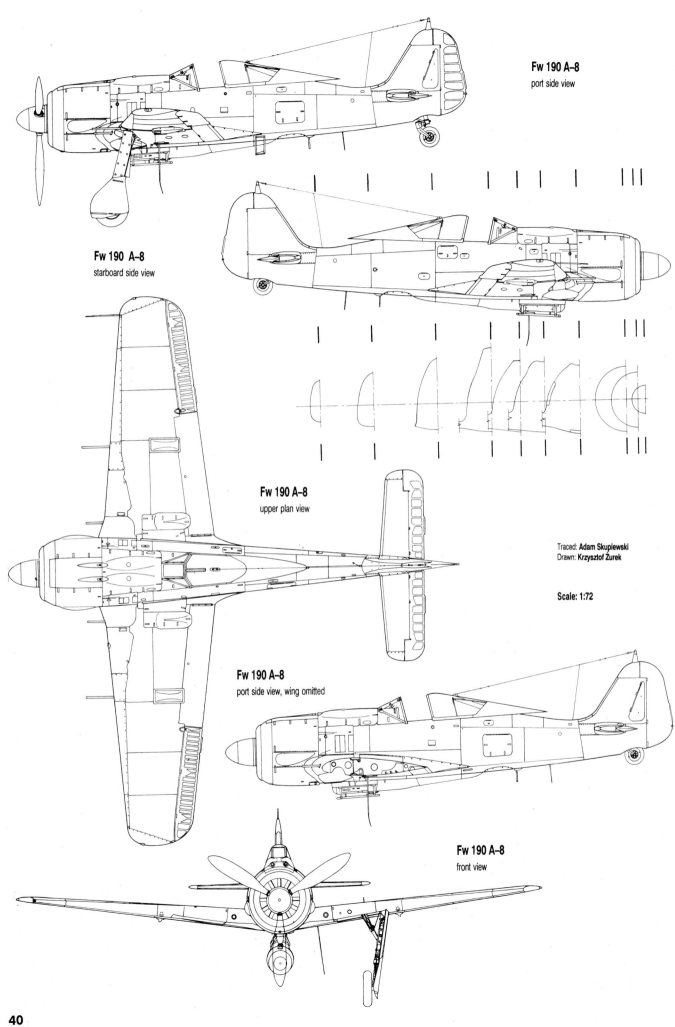

Fw 190 A–8
port side view

Fw 190 A–8
starboard side view

Fw 190 A–8
upper plan view

Traced: **Adam Skupiewski**
Drawn: **Krzysztof Żurek**

Scale: 1:72

Fw 190 A–8
port side view, wing omitted

Fw 190 A–8
front view

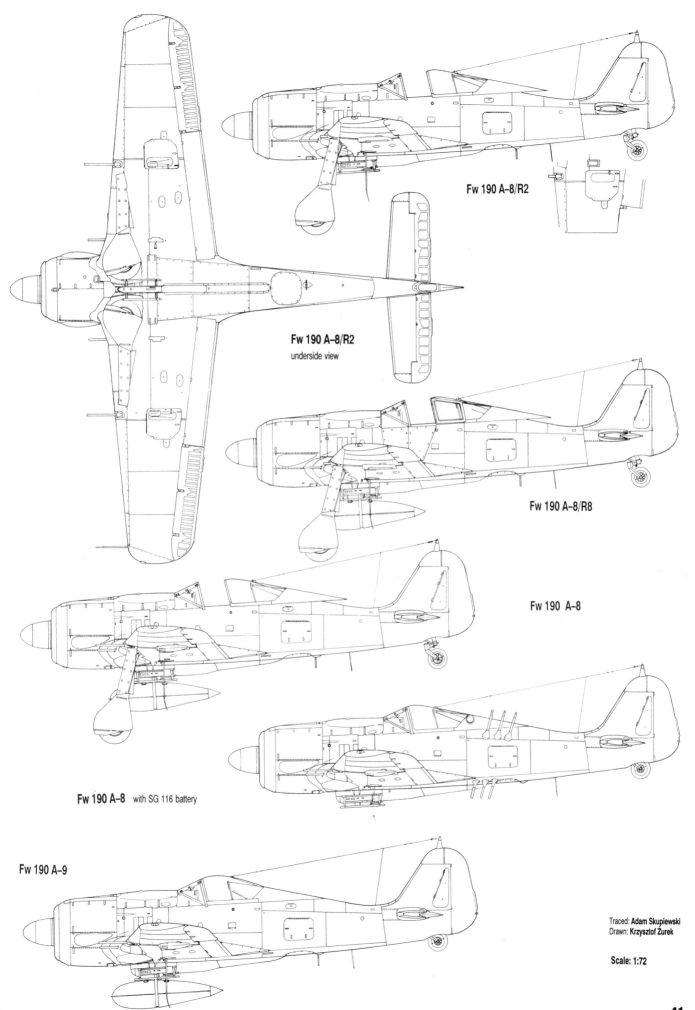

Fw 190 A–8/R2

Fw 190 A–8/R2
underside view

Fw 190 A–8/R8

Fw 190 A–8

Fw 190 A–8 with SG 116 battery

Fw 190 A–9

Traced: **Adam Skupiewski**
Drawn: **Krzysztof Żurek**

Scale: 1:72

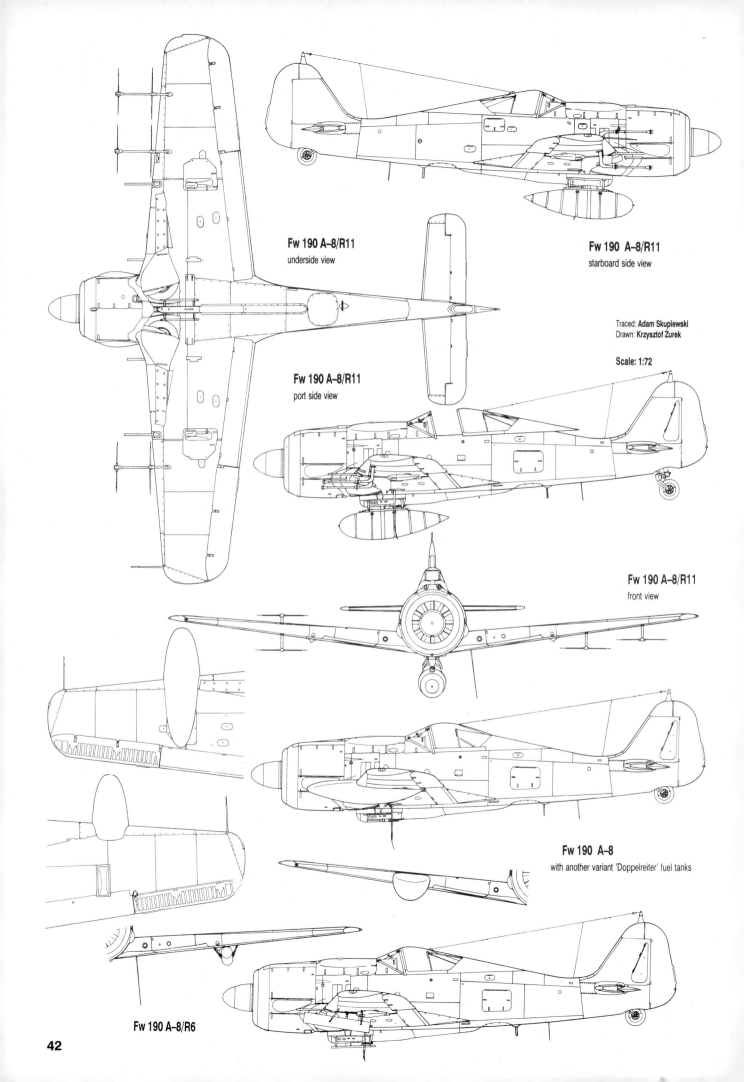

Fw 190 A–8/R11
underside view

Fw 190 A–8/R11
starboard side view

Traced: **Adam Skupiewski**
Drawn: **Krzysztof Żurek**

Scale: 1:72

Fw 190 A–8/R11
port side view

Fw 190 A–8/R11
front view

Fw 190 A–8
with another variant 'Doppelreiter' fuel tanks

Fw 190 A–8/R6

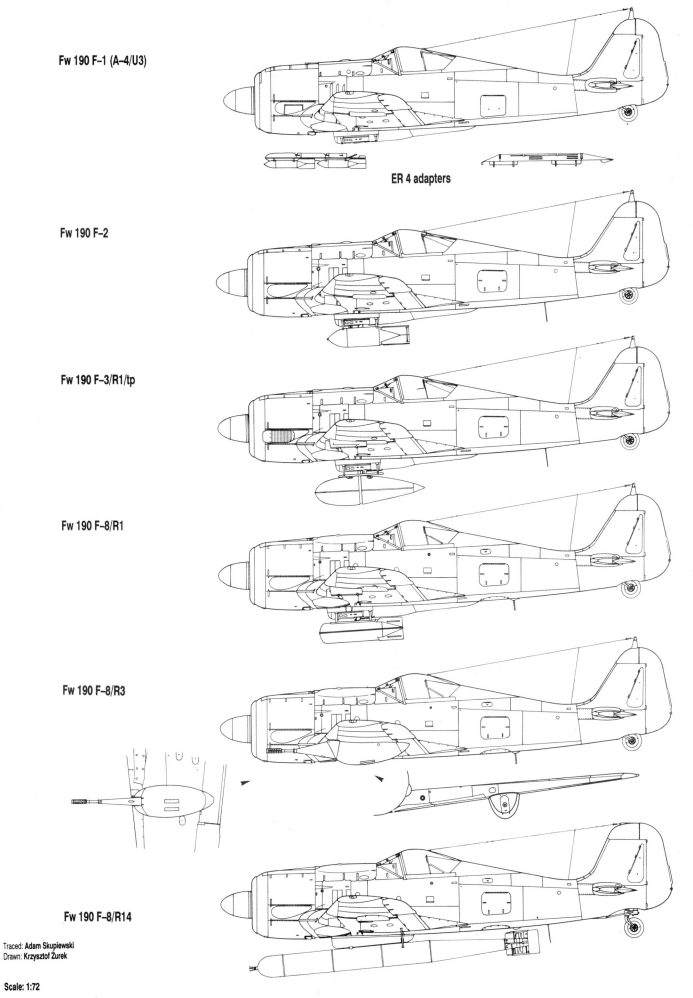

Fw 190 F–1 (A–4/U3)

ER 4 adapters

Fw 190 F–2

Fw 190 F–3/R1/tp

Fw 190 F–8/R1

Fw 190 F–8/R3

Fw 190 F–8/R14

Traced: **Adam Skupiewski**
Drawn: **Krzysztof Żurek**

Scale: 1:72

Fw 190 F–8/R16

with two BT 400

Fw 190 F–8/R16

with one BT 700

Fw 190 F–8

with Ruhrstahl X – 4 missiles

Fw 190 F–8

with W. Gr. 28/32 missiles

Fw 190 F–8

with SG 113 A Förstersonde launchers

Fw 190 F–9/Pb 1

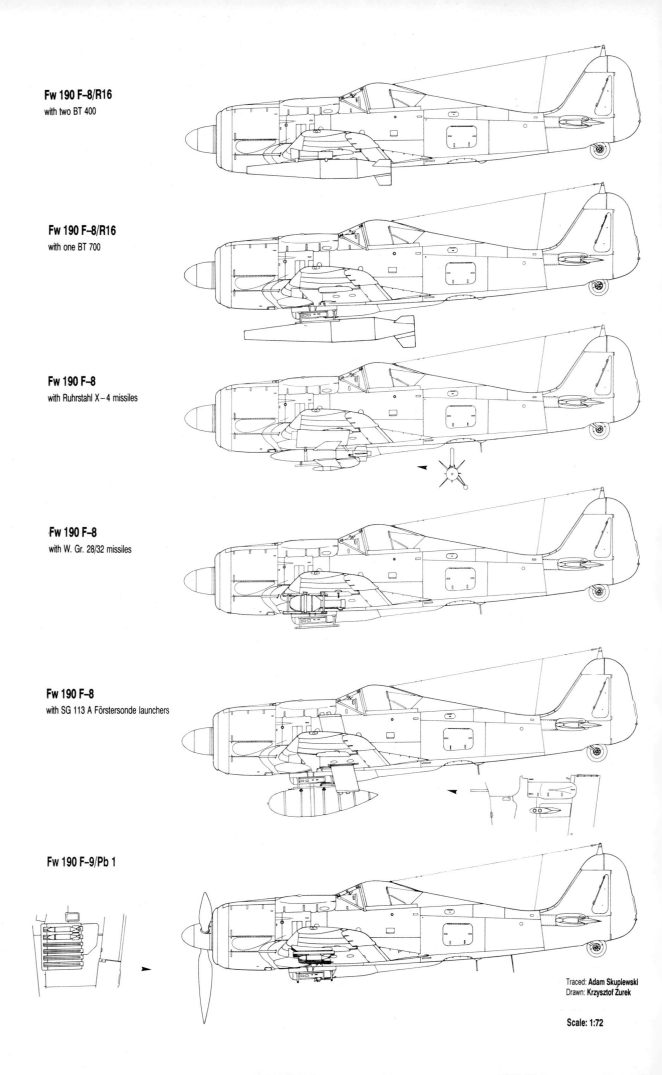

Traced: **Adam Skupiewski**
Drawn: **Krzysztof Żurek**

Scale: 1:72

Fw 190 G-1

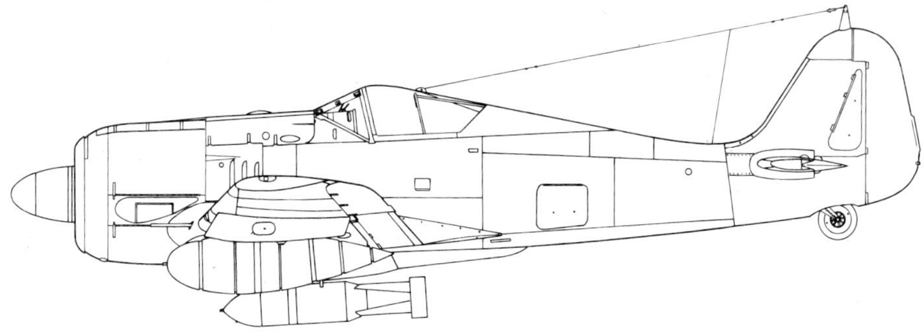

Fw 190 G-2
early version with V. Tr. – Ju 87

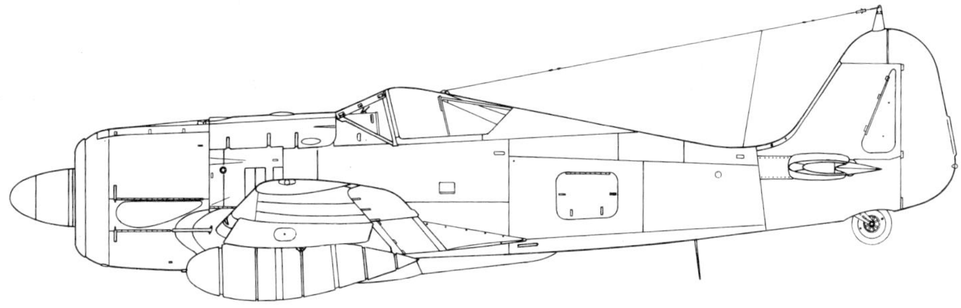

Fw 190 G-2

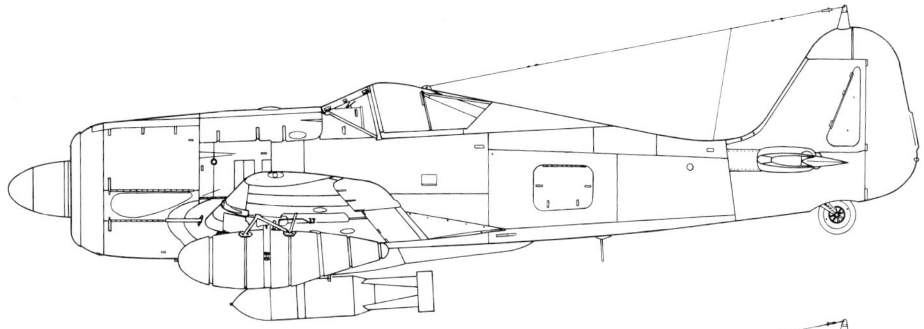

Fw 190 G-2/N

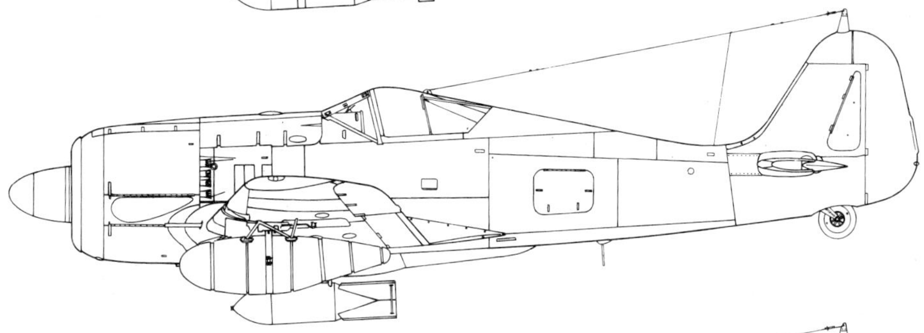

Fw 190 G-3

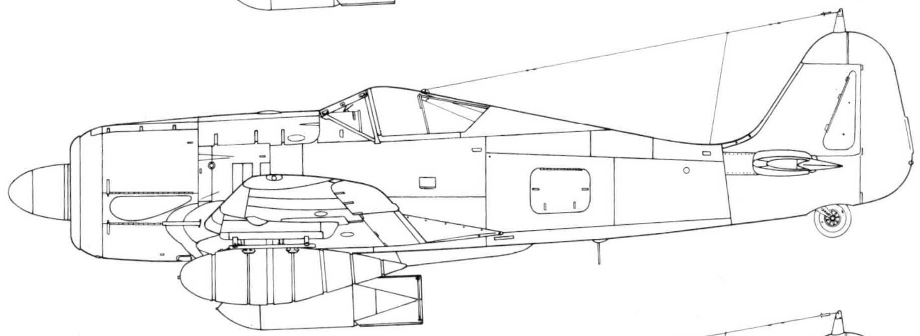

Fw 190 G-8

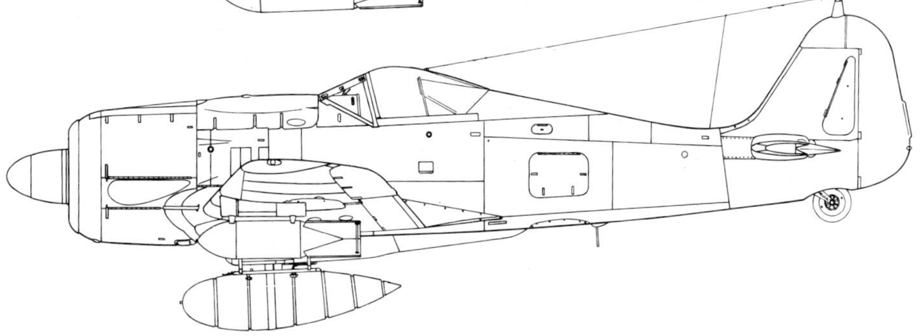

Traced: **Adam Skupiewski**
Drawn: **Krzysztof Żurek**

Scale: 1:72

CAMOUFLAGE & MARKINGS

Early Fw 190 A—0s at a factory airfield. The aircraft were painted RLM 02 Grau overall.

(MVT via M. Krzyżan)

First prototypes, the Fw 190 V1 and V2 were finished in the 1937—40 standard Luftwaffe scheme for fighters, bombers and most other types. The lower surfaces were painted RLM 65 Hellblau, while sides and upper surfaces were in a splinter, two—tone scheme of RLM 70 Schwarzgrün and RLM 71 Dunkelgrün. Some early prototypes and A—0 aircraft were painted overall RLM 02 Grau. The remaining A—0s and production aircraft were painted according to the new scheme, introduced for fighters first, and consisting of less contrasting grey shades, RLM 74 Dunkelgrau and RLM 75 Grauviolett, which formed a two—tone scheme on top surfaces, with soft and merged borders. Lower surfaces and sides were painted RLM 76 Lichtblau. In most cases the scheme received additional camouflage on sides, in the form of irregular areas in RLM 74, 75 or (less often, on early Fw 190s) RLM 02, 70.

In mid—1944 new RLM shades were introduced, to be used mainly on fighters. These were RLM 81 Braunviolett, 82 Dunkelgrün/Hellgrün and 83 Lichtgrün, all green shades, but since different manufacturers used different colouring agents the shades designated with the same number could differ widely. The general scheme remained unchanged, but the 74 was replaced with 82 or 83, and the side areas were painted 81 or 83. Careful study of photographs reveals that the upper surface pattern was not repeated exactly. Propeller spinners were painted RLM 71 at the factory. Fw 190

Fw 190 A—0, W.Nr. 0020, KB+PV, at the Bremen factory airfield. The aircraft already sports new camouflage of RLM 74/75/76.

(MVT via M. Krzyżan)

Fw 190 F — 2, winter 1943. The aircraft belonged to the II. Gruppe, probably of the SG 10. The camouflage is typical for the period.

(P. Jarrett via B. Ketley)

A—1s had 1/4 of the spinner painted RLM 21 white, while in service the spinner would usually be repainted in Staffel colour. The above rules applied to aircraft used in the ETO in temperate climate areas. Top surfaces of the aircraft used in the Eastern Front during winter were repainted with a washable white paint, while the Fw 190s of

JG 51 Mölders and JG 54 Grünherz, operating in the northern section of the Eastern Front, were painted in colours suitable for the area, i.e. top surfaces in 2—3 shades of

Fw 190 A — 4 of 8./JG 2, France, autumn 1942. Wing and tailplane camouflage scheme is well visible.

(P. Jarrett via B. Ketley)

Fw 190 A – 0 at a factory airfield. Note the radio call – sign on the fuselage and wing under – surface.

(MVT via M. Krzyżan)

green (mainly RLM 70 and 71, other shades were obtained by mixing in some RLM 04 Gelb or 25 Hellgrün).

Fw 190 Fs of the SG 4 operating in the Mediterranean were painted RLM 79 Sandgelb brown on top, with small areas of RLM 80 Olivegrün sprayed over it. Lower surfaces were at first painted RLM 78 Hellblau, later RLM 76. Fw 190 G fighter – bombers of SKG 10, used for night attacks against British Isles, had their lower surfaces painted black with a washable paint. Black permanent RLM 22 Schwarz paint was used on night fighting Fw 190s operating in 'Wilde Sau' tactics. The night fighters could also be RLM 75 grey on the top surfaces.

Aircraft used in operational units had their tactical numbers in the Staffel colour, and usually also the propeller spinner was in the same shade, often with a one – or two – colour spiral. Depending on the theatre of operations, quick identification markings were used, consisting of a band around the rear fuselage and areas in the wing – tips, lower engine cowling (often also the rudder) in yellow on the Russian Front and in white in the Mediterranean. However, it should be noted here that, for example, Fw 190s of JG 2 and JG 26 based in France had often their

rudders and lower engine cowlings in yellow, but lacked the yellow band around the rear fuselage and yellow wing – tips. In 1944 special two – or three – colour quick recognition bands around the rear fuselage were introduced in the Reichsverteidigung (Reich Defence) units, different for each unit. Most units also applied their emblems to the aircraft, either Geschwader, Gruppe, or Staffel ones, as well as individual pilot's badges.

Luftwaffe national markings consisting of a black cross of equal arms, the so – called Balkenkreuz, and the Hakenkreuz, or swastika. The markings were applied on both wing surfaces and fuselage sides (crosses) and on the fin (swastika) in entire or simplified form. Until 1943 the entire form dominated, with the cross and swastika in black with thin white and black outlines. Then the black outlines started to be omitted, leaving only the black markings with white outline. At the end of the war much simplified markings were used, consisting of only the white or black outline, or only the black or white cross/swastika without any outline. The colour depended on the background — dark on a light background, light on a dark one.

Fw 190 F – 8/R1 of an unidentified unit, spring 1945. Simplified national markings are evident.

(MVT via M. Krzyżan)

RLM STANDARD COLOURS

RLM 00 – Wasserhell (transparent)	RLM 67 – Dunkelolivgrün
	RLM 68 – Hellolivgrün
RLM 01 – Silber	RLM 69 – Lichtlohfarbe
RLM 02 – Grau (RLM Grau)	RLM 70 – Schwarzgrün
RLM 04 – Gelb	RLM 71 – Dunkelgrün
RLM 05 – Lasur	RLM 72 – Grün
RLM 21 – Weiß	RLM 73 – Grün
RLM 22 – Schwarz	RLM 74 – Dunkelgrau/Grüngrau
RLM 23 – Rot	
RLM 24 – Dunkelblau	RLM 75 – Grauviolet
RLM 25 – Hellgrün	RLM 76 – Lichtblau/Hellgrau
RLM 26 – Braun	RLM 77 – Hellgrau
RLM 27 – Gelb	RLM 78 – Hellblau
RLM 28 – Weinrot	RLM 79 – Sandgelb
RLM 41 – Grau	RLM 80 – Olivgrün
RLM 61 – Dunkelbraun	RLM 81 – Braunviolet/Dunkelgrün
RLM 62 – Grün	
RLM 63 – Grau (Lichtgrau/Grüngrau)	RLM 82 – Dunkelgrün/Hellgrün
RLM 64 – Lichtblau	RLM 83 – Lichtgrün
RLM 65 – Hellblau	RLM 99 – Gelbgrün
RLM 66 – Schwarzgrau	

SERVICE MARKINGS & STENCILLING
(diagram on the next page)

1	'Danger! Canopy drop explosive charge' – white letters on a red field. Upper row characters 25 mm high, two lower rows' characters – 15 mm high.
2	MW 50 system tank filler.
3	'Support here' – black characters 25 mm high.
4	'Incidence control indicator' – black characters 25 mm high
5	Factory number in black – size and shape of the characters would vary, depending on the factory.
6	'Support here' – black characters 25 mm high.
7	'Tyre pressure 5 atm' – black characters 25 mm high.
8	'Do not tamper' – white characters on a red background.
9	Indicator of the place were to attach rudder lock on the ground.
10	'Support here' – black characters 25 mm high.
11	Undercarriage position indicator – a protruding rod painted red on the upper half and white on the lower.
12	'Step here' – black characters 25 mm high.
13	Walking area marking – grey (RLM 77), or less often black, line of 20 x 10 mm segments.
14	'Luggage compartment'
15	First aid set compartment.
16	Socket for the external power supply on the ground.
17	'Oxygen' – white characters 5 mm high on a blue label. Fuselage fuel tank filler.
18	'Canopy – Open – Closed – press' – black characters 20 mm high.
19	Front fuselage fuel tank filler.
20	Shock – absorber pressure – two types of stencilling, characters 20 or 10 mm high.
21	'Tyre pressure 5,5 atm' – black characters 25 mm high.
22	